4-4-60

THE MUSICAL
PRODUCTION

THREE LITTLE MAIDS ("THE MIKADO")
(By courtesy of Bridget D'Oyly Carte)

THE MUSICAL PRODUCTION

A COMPLETE GUIDE FOR AMATEURS

BY

COSSAR TURFERY

AND

KING PALMER

LONDON
SIR ISAAC PITMAN & SONS, LTD.

First published 1953

SIR ISAAC PITMAN & SONS, Ltd.
PITMAN HOUSE, PARKER STREET, KINGSWAY, LONDON, W.C.2
THE PITMAN PRESS, BATH
PITMAN HOUSE, LITTLE COLLINS STREET, MELBOURNE
27 BECKETTS BUILDINGS, PRESIDENT STREET, JOHANNESBURG

ASSOCIATED COMPANIES
PITMAN PUBLISHING CORPORATION
2 WEST 45TH STREET, NEW YORK

SIR ISAAC PITMAN & SONS (CANADA), Ltd.
(INCORPORATING THE COMMERCIAL TEXT BOOK COMPANY)
PITMAN HOUSE, 381–383 CHURCH STREET, TORONTO

MADE IN GREAT BRITAIN AT THE PITMAN PRESS, BATH
E3—(G.420)

PREFACE

Of the many excellent books concerning the amateur stage there is none, we believe, which covers every aspect of amateur operatic stagecraft. It is our hope, therefore, that this book will usefully fill a gap in the theatrical bookshelf, and will assist amateur societies, large and small, in the production of light opera, musical comedy, pantomime, and revue.

In a book of this size it is obviously not possible to treat scenic design and construction, stage lighting, etc., in every detail, but specialized books devoted to these subjects already exist. Very full treatment has, however, been accorded to methods of production, and to the musical side; these matters, it seems to us, have so far never received the attention they deserve.

In the theatre, the main distinction between the professional and the amateur is that the professional practises the art for a livelihood while the amateur does it for pleasure. The professional has three advantages over the amateur—training, technique, and continuity of experience. The amateur player can only hope to acquire training and technique, in acting, singing or dancing, during his or her leisure hours. It is, therefore, going to take a considerable time for the amateur to reach professional standards in these respects. As for experience, this is intermittent in the amateur's case, and extends over an even longer period of time. Amateur productions are infrequent—two or three a year—whereas the successful professional is at it most of the time, rehearsing and acting.

On the other hand, there are compensations for the amateur. He does not have to depend upon the most uncertain and precarious of all professions for a livelihood. He can enjoy all the pleasure and satisfaction to be derived from an enjoyable hobby without any of the professional disadvantages. Given real enthusiasm, a good, if untrained, singing voice and, above all, a pleasing stage personality, he will find due reward in the pleasure he can bring to others through his artistic expression. Then, if the lure of the theatre proves too great he will find courage in the thought that many who have won success on the professional stage were once amateurs too.

Too much emphasis cannot be given to the importance of adequate rehearsal in amateur operatic productions. All society members should be made to realize the vast amount of work, both in organization and production, which must be expended by everyone concerned if a smooth and efficient show, approaching professional standards, is to result. Towards that end the intelligent amateur should study the professional at every opportunity—his acting, his technique, his stagecraft. He should look, listen, and absorb; learn, and keep on learning.

It is hoped that this book will prove a helpful guide to those engaged in amateur operatic production, and of interest to all whose hearts are in the theatre. In writing it, we have drawn on our experience, first as amateurs, and later as professionals in the world of entertainment. We have endeavoured to explain as simply as possible the main points in connexion with the formation and administration of an operatic society, and all the important aspects of production and musical interpretation.

In show business, whether it be amateur or professional, there is no one who can claim to know everything. It is with this reservation that we respectfully submit this volume for the guidance of our readers.

We gratefully acknowledge the help we have received from Norman Bidgood, Stanley Haig, Charles Henry, Earl Kay and James Shirvell, all of whom have made valuable suggestions. We are also indebted to Bridget D'Oyly Carte, Emile Littler, George Dance Musical Plays, Samuel French, Ltd., N.O.D.A., Scenic Display Services, Ltd., and Strand Electric and Engineering Co., Ltd., for their kind permission to use photographs, drawings and other material throughout the book; and to the Hornsey Operatic and Dramatic Society for allowing us to reproduce the rules of their Society.

COSSAR TURFERY
KING PALMER

CONTENTS

ix

CHAPTER TWELVE

CHAPTER THIRTEEN

CHAPTER FOURTEEN

CHAPTER FIFTEEN

CHAPTER SIXTEEN

CHAPTER SEVENTEEN

LIST OF ILLUSTRATIONS

CHAPTER ONE

THE FORMATION OF AN AMATEUR OPERATIC SOCIETY

THE urge to form an operatic society in a community emerges, as a rule, from the enthusiasm of a few individuals with a deep and sincere interest in music and the theatre. Enthusiasm is infectious and will soon attract others with a similar desire for artistic expression. There may be a few, of course, who will come along with the mistaken idea that it is going to be all fun and games and no work. They should be quickly disillusioned, and discouraged if necessary. Better to cut out the dead wood at the beginning than later.

Smaller localized groups, such as school and church societies, and societies attached to large organizations, public and private, like factories, big stores, corporations, youth organizations, etc., often have many advantages over the society which must find its members and its public without sponsorship of any kind. These advantages may include free rehearsal facilities, a hall or canteen suitable for stage performances without charge, space and facilities for making scenery, costumes, properties and so on, financial and other support from those in control, a choice of acting and musical talent within the organization, and very often an interested audience to draw upon as well. Not many societies enjoy all these advantages, and the new society which must make its own way will have to do a certain amount of intensive pioneering work before it becomes an established entity.

FIRST CONSIDERATIONS

The first thing to do is to make quite certain (a) that there is a large enough potential audience in the district to cover production costs which in the case of musical shows can be considerable; (b) that there are reasonable prospects of finding suitable musical and dramatic talent in the neighbourhood; (c) that adequate rehearsal facilities are available; and (d) that there is a theatre, well-equipped hall or cinema conveniently near where it is possible to stage musical shows effectively.

MAKING CONTACTS

Having checked up on the above points, the next thing to do is to make a few exploratory contacts before the first general meeting. It is at this meeting that the officers and committees of management will be elected.

In the course of these preliminary contacts it will be possible to gauge the prospects of running a society successfully in the area. It may be possible to get in touch with people who have been connected with the amateur movement in some other district. Their advice and guidance can be most helpful. The local theatre or cinema managers, too, are worth cultivating. Far from viewing a prospective amateur movement as an undesirable competitor they will, if they are astute, welcome it. Apart from the fact that the new society may use their premises for its productions, they should attract many new patrons through their co-operation and support.

There may be already in the district choral and orchestral societies which can sometimes provide not only a nucleus of first-class young singers but possibly an accompanist, a musical director, a chorus master, and a number of orchestral players of the requisite standard.

There are also the local schools of dancing and music where keen recruits will often be found. A good dancing school can usually provide an accomplished dance producer or ballet mistress as well as an efficient troupe and ballet.

As a rule, there is little difficulty in *forming* an operatic society. The important thing to avoid, in the early stages, is entering into premature commitments with individuals who only wish to use the new society for their own personal advertisement or profit. Every proposal made in the atmosphere of initial enthusiasm should be considered in the light of what is best for the society. The most capable musical director, the most imaginative and experienced dance producer, the most efficient secretary, the most reliable treasurer —all should be freely elected by a majority vote of members solely for their ability and sincere interest in the work and future of the movement.

ADMINISTRATION

The work involved in running an operatic society is considerable. When the preliminaries of formation have been disposed of, an administration should be set up to conduct the society's affairs. It must be a good administration, because no society can exist unless it pays its way. The composition of such an administration may vary in detail in different societies, but as a rule it will include a President, a Chairman, a Secretary, a Treasurer, and a Public Relations Officer to look after the society's publicity.

The President

The most distinguished and influential personality in the vicinity should be invited to become President. The acceptance of this office by the right person can prove of immense value to a society. A benevolent interest on his part in the society's work will reflect itself in the smoothing out of many difficulties, in obtaining special facilities and other benefits to be derived from the prestige and local influence he can bring to bear on the society's behalf.

The Chairman

The Chairman should be chosen for his tact, firmness, and capacity to handle meetings and committee business with impartiality and dispatch.

The Secretary

The Secretary is the negotiating official of the society, and its business manager. He carries out its decisions, conducts its correspondence, and enters into contracts on its behalf. Some societies have separate appointments for Business Manager and Secretary.

The Treasurer

The Treasurer is the society's Chancellor of the Exchequer. He is in complete control of its finances, and prepares all the estimates of production cost and possible box office returns. After each production he prepares a detailed balance sheet showing the financial result. He will do this in conjunction with the society's auditors if this service is available. It is a vital office, difficult to fill, and far removed from the glamour of the stage.

Solicitors and Auditors

It is usual nowadays for larger societies to have honorary solicitors and auditors. Many societies enjoy considerable benefits from the services provided freely by local firms prepared to interest themselves in the amateur movement in their district.

Public Relations

Public relations, i.e. publicity in its widest sense, is an essential part of the organization of a progressive operatic society. A member in the printing, publishing or advertising business, or a publicity executive from a local firm, will very often be prepared to act as the society's honorary public relations officer. The important part he can play in the society's affairs is dealt with in detail in the next chapter.

PRODUCTION STAFF

Apart from the Producer, a fully representative production staff for a large operatic society might include—

Musical Director	Art Director
Chorus Master and Deputy	Property Master
Musical Director	Mistress of the Robes
Dance Producer	Master of the Robes
Accompanist (and Assistant)	Make-up Artist
Stage Manager	Hairdresser
Assistant Stage Manager	Prompter
Electrician	Call Boy
Carpenter	

Smaller societies, working within more modest limits, may not, of course, require such a large staff to handle their productions. Some of the duties may be combined, e.g. musical director, chorus master, and accompanist; stage manager, electrician, and carpenter; and so on. Whatever modifications are made to the staff as described, however, their total responsibilities remain the same.

The duties and responsibilities of the production staff are fully described in later chapters.

COMMITTEES

An executive committee should be appointed as soon as possible to carry out in detail the resolutions and decisions of the society. As the society's activities develop, it will be necessary to form sub-committees to deal exclusively with particular aspects of the work, e.g. social events, production details, and so on. Such sub-committees usually have their own secretaries, thereby taking much work off the shoulders of the general secretary.

SUBSCRIPTIONS

Fixing the amount of a new society's subscriptions is always a difficult problem. It depends largely on what the members in a particular district can afford on the average. If the subscription is rated too low it may attract more members, but it may also produce a tendency to undervalue membership among certain elements in the society. If, on the other hand, it is fixed too high it may deprive the society of much good talent by discouraging many potential members on grounds of expense.

The society must pay its way. The subscriptions should at least cover the running expenses, as distinct from the production costs which must be met from returns from the society's social activities—dances, concerts, whist drives, etc.—and from the sale of tickets for its productions. The amount of the subscription, therefore, should be fixed with all these considerations in mind.

Some societies make a weekly charge instead of an annual subscription, and this is usually considered an easier method of collection. In the case of honorary or non-acting members, subscriptions often entitle them to one, or two, complimentary tickets for each show.

RULES

The rules of a society should provide for all possible eventualities. The following rules of the Hornsey Operatic and Dramatic Society, which has been in operation for over twenty-five years, indicate the various points which ought to be observed when drafting the rules of a new society.

1. The Society shall be called "The Hornsey Operatic and Dramatic Society."

2. The objects of the Society shall be the cultivation of the Arts of Music and Drama, particularly among the youth of the District, the encouragement of public appreciation of those arts, and the raising of funds for charitable and philanthropic purposes.

3. The Society shall consist of Patrons, President, Vice-Presidents, Acting, Student, Honorary, and Life Members, the last named being members (nominated by the Committee and elected at a General Meeting) who have rendered special services to the Society, and such membership allowing the same privileges as those enjoyed by Acting Members, but not involving the same obligations, unless the member is actually taking part in the production. The Patrons, President, Vice-Presidents, Student, and Honorary Members shall also be exempt from financial obligations resulting from losses incurred on productions.

3a. The Mayor of Hornsey shall be invited to accept the office of President during his period of Mayoralty; but, should he be unable to accept the office, the position shall be filled according to the wishes of the Society.

3b. The Vice-Presidents may be elected at a General Meeting.

4. The Society shall be managed by a Committee consisting of the following Officers, viz: Secretary, Business Manager, Treasurer, Publicity Manager, Ticket Secretary, Honorary Members' Secretary, Chairman, and five Acting Members. Any two offices can be combined at the discretion of the Society.

5. The election or expulsion of a member, or members, other than Life Members, for any reason whatsoever, shall rest solely with the Committee.

6. All members shall be required to sign the approved form of membership agreeing to abide by the Rules of the Society.

7. Prior to election, all candidates for Acting Membership shall satisfy the Committee as to their vocal, dancing, or histrionic ability.

8. The Entrance Fee to the Society, applying only to Acting Membership, shall be 10s. 6d., and payable immediately on election to membership.

8a. The subscription to the Society for Acting Members shall be at the rate of 1s. 6d. per week, payable weekly, except during the four weeks of summer recess.

8b. The subscription for Honorary Membership shall be 15s. per annum.

9. The financial year of the Society shall end on 31st July; the annual Profit and Loss Account and Balance Sheet shall be prepared and presented to the Committee within three calendar months after that date.

10. MEMBERS wishing to resign must give written notice to the Secretary; in default of so doing they will be liable for the weekly subscription. In the event of a member being unable to take part in a production, and his or her reasons being acceptable to the Committee, the Committee shall, at their discretion, suspend such membership, and no further entrance fee will be required on rejoining.

11. The Annual General Meeting of the Society shall be held in December, when the Report of the Committee and the Accounts for the past year, duly audited, shall be presented; the Officers and other members of the Committee, and two Auditors for the ensuing year, elected; and all general business transacted.

12. An Extraordinary General Meeting of the Society may be called at any time at the discretion of the Committee. Such Meeting can also be called within twenty-one days after receipt by the Secretary of a requisition in writing to that effect, signed by at least twelve Acting Members. Any such requisition shall specify the business for which the meeting is to be convened, and no other business shall be transacted at that Meeting.

13. No business other than the formal adjournment of the meeting shall be transacted at any General Meeting unless a quorum be present, and such quorum shall consist of not less than twenty-five persons present and entitled to vote.

14. UNLESS otherwise provided by these Rules, all resolutions brought forward at a General Meeting shall be decided by a bare majority of the votes properly recorded at such meeting, and in the case of an equality of votes the Chairman shall have the second or casting vote.

15. The Committee, including the Officers and Auditors, shall retire annually, and shall be eligible for re-election. If all the before-mentioned positions shall not be filled at the Annual General Meeting, or any vacancy shall thereafter occur, the Committee shall be empowered to fill such vacancy. No Member serving on the Committee of any other Operatic Society shall be eligible for election to the Committee.

16. A written notice of the Annual General Meeting, accompanied by a statement of the Accounts for the past financial year, shall be sent to each member at least fourteen days prior to the date fixed for such meeting. In the case of an Extraordinary General Meeting, at least seven days' notice shall be given.

17. The Committee shall have power to appoint Sub-Committees and to delegate to such sub-committees any of its powers. Such sub-committees may be dissolved at the discretion of the Committee.

18. The Chairman, Secretary, and Treasurer shall be ex-officio members of all sub-committees.

19. The cast for any production shall be selected by a Selection Committee, which shall consist of—

(*a*) Three persons (other than Acting Members) selected by the General Committee for their knowledge and experience.

(*b*) One member of the General Committee elected by that Committee.

(*c*) Three Acting Members elected by the General Body of Members.

(*d*) Producer and Musical Director who shall be entitled to vote provided both are present.

Four members of the Selection Committee shall constitute a quorum. The Chairman of the General Committee shall be the Chairman of the Selection Committee.

The findings of the Selection Committee shall be approved by the General Committee before announcement is made to the Society.

The General Committee shall have power to cast any parts not decided by the Selection Committee, to revise the cast from time to time if any acting member to whom a character has been assigned shall, in its opinion, prove unsuitable for the part, and to recast any part becoming vacant for any reason whatsoever.

20. The General Committee may appoint a Special Committee for the selection of Dancers consisting of such suitable persons as they may think fit.

21. The Musical Director shall conduct and control all Musical rehearsals, and the Producer shall control all Stage rehearsals.

22. All Members are expected to attend rehearsals regularly. The Committee shall have the power to suspend or expel a member who is consistently absent or late at rehearsals without a satisfactory explanation being given to the Secretary.

23. The Committee shall from time to time submit to the General Meeting at least three works recommended for production, and the General Meeting shall select from such works one to be produced. Voting on the production shall take place one week after notification of the three shows has been given to the General Body. Only Acting Members shall vote on the choice of a production.

24. EACH and every Acting Member shall be deemed to be liable in equal shares for any losses or debts incurred. All monies due and owing to the Society, including subscriptions, shall be recoverable at law in the name of the Secretary.

25. The first meeting of the Committee shall be called by the Secretary, and shall be held within twenty-one days after the Annual General Meeting. All subsequent Meetings of the Committee shall be called by the Secretary in accordance with

any resolution to that effect passed by the Committee, and failing any such resolution, at the discretion of the Chairman and Secretary. Five shall form a quorum.

26. The Committee shall have power to decide any questions arising out of these Rules and all other matters connected with the Society (other than those which can only be dealt with by the Society in General Meeting), and make and maintain and publish all necessary orders, regulations and bye-laws in connexion therewith.

27. A Social Committee consisting of at least six Members shall be elected at the Annual General Meeting. They shall be responsible for the social activities of the Society, and shall notify the Secretary of the Society of all functions arranged. They shall appoint their own officers and keep their own accounts, which shall be submitted to the Auditors, but shall not incur any liability in the name of the Society without the sanction of the General Committee. The Social Committee may fill all casual vacancies or co-opt other members.

28. EXCEPT where otherwise stated or inferred, the term Committee used herein shall refer to the General Committee.

28a. The name of the Society shall not be publicly used or advertised for any purpose whatsoever without the approval of the General Committee.

29. The Funds of the Society shall be applied solely to the stated objects of the Society. No member of the Society shall receive payment directly or indirectly for services to the Society or for other than legitimate expenses incurred in its work. In the event of dissolution of the Society the remaining funds shall be devoted to objects similar to those of the Society, or to other purposes approved by the Commissioners of Customs and Excise.

30. The Society shall only be dissolved by resolution passed by at least five-sixths of the members present and voting at a special General Meeting called for the purpose of considering such dissolution.

31. No alteration of these Rules shall be made except at a General Meeting or unless 21 days prior to such meeting a written notice of the proposed alteration, or of one substantially to the like effect, shall have been given to the Secretary, who shall give 14 days' notice thereof to the Members, and the resolution embodying such proposed alteration shall be carried by at least two-thirds of the votes recorded thereon at the Meeting.

These are the rules of a large society with many fine productions to its credit and are based on an administrative experience extending over many years. They are designed to cover every possible eventuality and should serve as a useful basis for new societies, large and small, when drafting their rules.

ENCOURAGING LOCAL SUPPORT

The work of an amateur operatic society is closely bound up with the social life of the community. Every member, with the support of an enthusiastic and hard-working committee of management, should be prepared to play his or her part in enlisting new acting and honorary members. A long list of honorary members means more money in the box office through the sale of tickets. An explanatory leaflet, setting out the aims and forthcoming productions of the society, is useful for publicizing its activities and increasing the number of members, acting and honorary. An application form for membership should be incorporated in this leaflet.

The social committee should set about organizing dances, concerts and other attractions to stimulate local interest generally. An amateur society, particularly a new one, should never allow itself to become moribund. Something should always be going on from one year's end to the other. Only in this way can the interest of its members, and its public, be maintained.

The production of a concert version of a well-known light opera or other suitable work, with plenty of good choral singing, is an excellent way of showing the public what the new society can do on the vocal side. Permission, of course, must be obtained from the publishers of the work, and the necessary fees allowed for. A concert version can be performed without costumes or scenery; it must, however, be well presented. It should be adequately advertised in the local Press, which will generally lend a helping hand in this respect through its editorial columns. Local factories, big stores, schools, colleges, and all centres where groups of people are concentrated should be approached, if possible by personal contact. Shops will display posters, and music shops will co-operate in the sale of tickets. Newsagents are often willing to enclose leaflets with their newspaper deliveries, especially if they are honorary members of the society.

The possibilities of publicity are considerable, and a resourceful and energetic Public Relations Officer will soon find ways and means of advertising the society's activities at little cost beyond printing, postages, and the judicious allocation of a limited number of complimentary tickets.

A concert version of a light opera should be presented on an adequately-lit stage or concert platform. Additional lighting should be introduced if necessary to give the production something of the warmth and atmosphere of a theatre even although it is not being performed in one. During the performance the house lights should be lowered leaving a concentration of stage or platform lighting on the singers. Evening dress should be worn, and if the ladies can all wear white the choral grouping can be most effective. The singing principals need not, of course, follow this uniformity.

An orchestra is desirable, but if it is not available good results can often be obtained from one (or two) grand pianos, or from a cinema or other organ.

Care should be taken with the layout and printing of the programmes, which can contain information about the society and an announcement concerning its first operatic production. An application form for acting and honorary members can also be included in the programme. After the interval, before the second half of the programme, a *short* talk on the aims and plans of the society may be given by the President or Chairman, with an appeal for local support and members.

Variety concerts can also be organized on similar lines at small expense. They are useful for attracting new acting and singing members if a talent competition is included in the programme.

Another good idea for filling in the gap during the new society's early existence is to stage a non-musical play. Many established operatic societies, of course, do this as part of their production programme.

The important thing is to keep the society constantly in the public eye so that it quickly becomes recognized as an active and virile force in the social and artistic life of the community. At the end of the first twelve months of its existence, the new society should be able to look back on a useful period of pioneer work, culminating in its first operatic stage production with plans already laid for the second.

CHAPTER TWO

PUBLIC RELATIONS

THE society's Public Relations Officer (P.R.O. for short) should begin his work the moment the show has been decided upon.

EDITORIAL PUBLICITY

His first job will be to draft news paragraphs to appear in the editorial columns of the local press and other suitable media. There may be large factories and other big organizations in the district with house and staff magazines, and they often appreciate news of local interest for publication in their columns.

In drafting his publicity material the P.R.O. should, if the society is producing a well-known work, find out as much as he can about the original production of the work and its subsequent history. At which famous theatre was it first produced? Who were the stars? Which members of the society are playing their parts? Did it enjoy an exceptional run? Who produced it? Did a famous composer of light music conduct it? What are the most popular tunes? Who wrote the book? What is the story and the setting? These are the news items the public like to read about, linked up with any relevant society information of local interest.

If the society is doing an entirely new show for the first time, the approach will be different. The P.R.O. will want all the information he can obtain about the author or composer. Is it their first work? Are they well known in other fields of writing and music? A few words about the story and setting should be included and, if the music is already published, a special window display can usually be arranged at the local music shops. What outstanding feature of the show influenced the society's decision to produce it?

The P.R.O. must, of course, embellish his facts so as to give them journalistic value. The theatre and film gossip columns of the national press and magazines provide a good working pattern for style and conciseness. Plain accuracy can be dull. Editorial publicity should be brief, bright, and breezy.

There will be further opportunities for publicity in the press when the show has been cast and a producer appointed. Photographs of the leading players should be sent to the press nearer the opening performance of the show.

There may be good news stories of local interest in the personalities of the amateur artists who will be playing the leading parts. Who are they? Are they barristers, miners, teachers, business executives, bankers, typists, nurses? Whatever their walk of life there is a story line to be culled from what, very often, appears dull and commonplace on the surface.

Another good publicity angle is to invite a number of distinguished people, local and otherwise, to become vice-presidents of the society. A few of the interested ones will agree. They may be film, stage, radio or television stars, sporting personalities, or well-known figures in music and art. An announcement in the press of their appointment will provide an interesting piece of news publicity for the society. If possible, photographs should accompany the notice.

The society's P.R.O. should aim at issuing story bulletins to the press at reasonable intervals and so keep public interest alive. Successful publicity depends upon cumulative effect and the skill with which well-planned editorial information, press advertising, and the distribution of printed matter are used to supplement each other to the best effect.

PRESS ADVERTISING

The press advertisements for the show should be bold, simple, and straightforward. They should also be given adequate space. It is better to have a few six- or eight-inch double-column insertions, or even larger spaces according to the rate, than a number of small, crowded advertisements. The copy should be confined to essentials including the name of the theatre, cinema or hall in which the show is taking place, the name of the society, the length of the run, the times of the performances, the title of the show, prices of admission and where tickets may be obtained. If the work is by a famous composer, his name should be boldly featured. A line drawing applicable to the show will attract attention, and particular care should be taken with the layout and general presentation.

PRINTED MATTER

If the society has appointed an honorary Art Director, he can contribute usefully to the preparation of programmes, hand-bills, show cards, and posters. If the P.R.O. is an experienced publicity man he will be responsible for the copy, layout, and typography. Together they can devise a characteristic style which should become identified with the artistic standards of the society. Attractive stock blocks in black and white and colour for use with all types of theatrical publicity are obtain-able from firms specializing in this work. A well-designed illustration provides an effective visual link which should be featured in all forms of printed matter, press advertisements, posters, box-office cards, leaflets, programmes, etc.

If the show is being presented in a theatre the usual poster sites and outlets for printed matter and showcards will be available to the society. Otherwise the local billposting firm should be approached about sites, and posters ordered accordingly.

Small bills or showcards should be supplied to shops, public houses, hotels, institutes, factories, and other sites arranged by the P.R.O.

Throwaways, or handbills, can be in the usual 2-page form, or better still in the form of a more explanatory 4-page leaflet including an order form for tickets on the back especially for prospective patrons in outlying districts. These leaflets can also be used for postal publicity, and considerable business can be obtained through a properly planned campaign.

SLIDE ADVERTISING

Slide announcements can, as a rule, be arranged with the theatre in which the show is being presented so that they appear during the week or fortnight preceding the production. The local cinemas may also co-operate, although it might not appear to be in their interest to do so. It should be remembered, however, that many of the members of the society and its patrons are also the patrons of the cinema, and managers will usually take the long view when faced with a request to advertise a rival attraction of this kind.

PROMOTIONAL IDEAS

Sometimes it may be possible to interest national advertisers in supplying materials for the show, and linking this up with window displays in the local shops to advertise the show before and during its run. Dress fabrics, furnishings, and other suitable goods widely advertised in the Press can often be obtained free on loan in return for programme advertising. The window displays can include matter relating to the show and photographs of the leading principals.

A loud-speaker van or car from which announcements about the show can be broadcast is one of the most effective methods of advertisement. A wide area can be covered in a comparatively short time. The announcement should be brief and to the point—the name of the show and where and when it is being played is enough. This idea is particularly useful as a last-minute "boost" for any performances where bookings are not up to expectations.

Another good promotional idea is to enlist the co-operation of the local motor-coach companies, and arrange for parties from outlying districts at an inclusive charge to cover the fare, a meal on arrival, and seats for the show.

Members of the Society should be invited to suggest ideas for publicity. An appeal of this kind may reveal some useful contact or advertising channel which otherwise might never have come to light. Members with cars and other motor vehicles, for example, might volunteer to fix to their windscreens and rear windows printed strips advertising the show.

Some ideas can be *too* clever, as in the case of one enterprising society which hit upon the bright notion of using ordinary post cards for a circularizing scheme. On the back, in plain homely handwriting, were the words MEET ME TO-NIGHT AT SEVEN OUTSIDE THE GRAND THEATRE. LOVE, GEORGE. Several thousands of these were duplicated and addressed, also in handwriting, to residential districts throughout the town. The results were highly satisfactory, except for the protests received from some irate recipients complaining bitterly of domestic strife, broken engagements, and impending separations.

CHAPTER THREE

SOME MATTERS FOR CONSIDERATION

THE newly-formed operatic society would do well to consider the advantage to be derived from affiliation to a national organization devoted to the interests of such amateur societies.

N.O.D.A.

The National Operatic and Dramatic Association, established in 1899, is the only organization of its kind which devotes its energies to every phase of the amateur musical and dramatic stage in Great Britain and overseas. Its policy is to improve production standards, promote friendly intercourse between its members, encourage creative work, obtain concessions for its members, and protect their interests in every way.

In a little more than fifty years the Association has grown from a small nucleus of thirty societies to a membership of over one thousand. It consists of (a) Operatic and Dramatic Societies, Clubs, and Companies, and (b) Individual Members interested in operatic and dramatic art. The Head Office of the Association in London possesses a comprehensive library of over 30,000 volumes comprising marked stage books, vocal scores, libretti, dramatic works, pictorials, and a unique collection of general literature relating to the stage. This library is available for the use of societies and members, and books and scores may be obtained on payment of moderate deposits and hiring fees. There is also an orchestral library, generously gifted to the Association by the Carnegie United Kingdom Trust, from which musical scores can be hired by amateur orchestras and all members at low fees.

The Association offers, in return for a very reasonable subscription, many benefits, including free legal advice, insurance schemes at advantageous premiums, the provision of professional producers, critics and adjudicators, of substitute players in cases of emergency, free use of the libraries, protection against excessive charges, advice on taxation, free criticism of original plays and musical works, and many other advantages too numerous to set out in detail here.

The N. O. D. A. Bulletin, issued periodically, contains the latest information on all amateur and Association matters, including a fixture list of forthcoming productions by affiliated societies.

The N. O. D. A. Year Book, issued on loan to each affiliated society, contains a wealth of information on legal matters, entertainments duty, income tax, licensing of plays and theatres, copyright, and other matters of vital interest connected with amateur administration and progress.

The value of affiliation to a national organization of this kind is obvious, especially to a new society. Full information on the aims and objects of the Association and the advantages of membership can be obtained from the Director, National Operatic and Dramatic Association, 8 Bernard Street, London, W.C.1.

THEATRE REGULATIONS

Theatres and other places of public entertainment are subject to local regulations. These vary throughout the country and are enforced for the safety of the public. The society should acquaint itself with these regulations before performances are given.

The most common risk is fire. For this reason all scenery, curtains, inflammable properties such as artificial flowers, etc., must be rendered fireproof by painting them with a solution made from fireproof crystals obtainable from theatrical suppliers or local stores.

All scenery is subject to examination at any time by an inspector from the local authority. He can test the efficiency of the fireproofing by holding a flame against the canvas or other material. If it does not burst into flame, but merely smoulders, the proofing will be passed as efficient. Otherwise, he will insist on the whole job being carried out before any performance takes place.

Fireproof solution remains effective for a limited period of time only. Most contractors see that their scenery is properly proofed before it goes out, but if there is any doubt the society should obtain an assurance that it has been tested and passed as fireproof. The same applies to draperies and curtains, and if any of these items have been purchased or hired locally they must be similarly treated.

Naked flame, such as a lighted candle, must not be used on the stage. The effect must be obtained electrically.

Other regulations deal with exits from the auditorium and from the stage. All exits must be kept clear. Objection will be raised immediately to any scenery, furniture, or other properties placed in such a position as to interfere with ready access to the stage exit doors, particularly emergency exits.

Permission should be obtained well in advance if firearms or effects involving explosives are used.

All wooden structures such as rostrums, steps, staircases, and so on must be soundly built so that they are safe and will continue to be so under hard use. Steps and approaches to rostrums off stage should be properly constructed, and make-shift devices like wooden boxes, shaky chairs and tables, etc., avoided.

THE LAW OF COPYRIGHT

Royalties are payable on all copyright musical plays. Copyright covers music, libretto, and lyrics, and subsists during the life of the author or composer, and for fifty years after death. In the case of a work published posthumously, the period is fifty years, either from the date of publication or from the first performance, whichever is the earlier.

Although the music of a show may be out of copyright because the composer has been dead for more than fifty years, it does not follow that the complete work is out of copyright. The authors of the libretto and lyrics may still be alive or, if dead, the terms of copyright may not have expired. In this case royalties are still payable for public performances of the complete work. The Gilbert and Sullivan operas are an example of this. The music of Sullivan is out of copyright, but the libretto and lyrics of Gilbert are not, and royalties must be paid on all occasions when the complete operas are performed.

Most composers and authors in this country are members of the Performing Rights Society. Theatres, cinemas, certain halls, and other premises are licensed by the Society for the performance of songs and music written and composed by its members. Premises thus licensed pay an annual fee to the

Society so that songs and musical items (but *not* complete musical plays or light operas) can be performed without further payment. Every item thus performed, however, must be entered on a record sheet by those responsible for the performance, and returned to the Society. The total revenue derived from premises licensed in this way is shared out among the Society's members.

Public performances of full-length copyright musical plays and light operas are always subject to the payment of royalties. Before publicly performing a copyright work of any description, therefore, societies should always apply for permission to the publishers or copyright owners concerned. The public performance, without permission or payment, of any copyright work subject to royalties renders those responsible liable to prosecution.

COSTING A MUSICAL PRODUCTION

Excess of artistic zeal should not be permitted to obscure the economic side of amateur operatic production, and it is important for the administration of the society's affairs to be in capable hands.

There are many items which are liable to be overlooked when costing a musical show, and to embark upon production without a clear and detailed estimate is to court disaster.

Cost items will vary according to whether the show is being produced in a theatre with full facilities or in a hall with few; whether the resident stage and theatre staff, box-office arrangements, publicity, billposting, etc., are included in the hire or rental agreement; whether entertainment tax is payable or not, and other factors.

A complete cost statement should be prepared in accordance with the prevailing conditions, and approved by the management committee before contracts are entered into on behalf of the society. Such a cost statement, or budget, will include the following items—

1. Rehearsal accommodation.
2. Hire or purchase of vocal scores and libretti.
3. Royalties.
4. Hire or rental of theatre, cinema or hall.
5. Cost of dress rehearsal, including stage staff, electricians, etc.
6. Salaries of professional musicians.
7. Other salaries—stage and front of the house.
8. Hire of scenery, including extra equipment, e.g. tab rails, curtains, and drapes not available in the building.
9. Hire of costumes.

10. Local purchase or hire of modern costumes.
11. Hire of wigs.
12. Hire of furniture.
13. Hire and purchase of properties.
14. Make-up and hairdressing.
15. Hire of additional lighting equipment.
16. Hire of music stands, lights, orchestra rail and curtains, piano, etc.
17. Hire of band parts.
18. Printing: Posters. Handbills. Tickets, Programmes. Photographs. Display Cards. Stationery.
19. Publicity: Poster space. Press advertising. Postage on circulars. Special schemes.
20. Entertainment tax.
21. Transport of equipment.
22. Gratuities.
23. Producer's fee.
24. Dance Producer's fee.
25. Entertaining for business purposes.
26. Musical Director's honorarium.
27. Insurance.[1]

The foregoing list covers the main cost items likely to arise in the production of a musical show. To the smaller society it may appear formidable. Many items may not apply, however. The Producer and Musical Director, for example, may both be members of the society and willing to work without payment of a fee or honorarium. The society may make its own scenery and costumes. Rehearsal accommodation may be freely available. Whatever the circumstances the important thing in estimating is to make sure that nothing has been left out. Items of expenditure have a habit of cropping up unexpectedly unless a careful budget is prepared. It is a good idea, when preparing a budget, to allow in addition a safety margin of ten per cent of the total estimate to meet any eventualities which may arise.

ENTERTAINMENT TAX

Entertainment duty is payable on all public performances of musical plays for which admission is charged, but exemption may be granted by the Commissioners of Customs and Excise to societies who devote their proceeds to charity. Exemption is *not* automatically conferred by the law and must be granted by the Commissioners *for each entertainment*, and application should be made at least fourteen days before the entertainment is held. An explanatory leaflet describing the conditions for exemption and full information can be obtained from the Secretary, Customs and Excise, City Gate House, Finsbury Square, London, E.C.2.

[1] A Combined Policy should be taken out covering wardrobe, scenery, properties and furniture, electrical and other equipment hired by the Society; transit risks; members' personal clothing and properties during the run of the show; employers' liability for accidents to all employed persons, including casual labour; and third-party risks.

CHAPTER FOUR

CHOOSING A MUSICAL SHOW

In choosing a musical show there are three important factors to be considered:

1. Will it please the audience?
2. Will it please the members?
3. Is it practicable?

FIRST CONSIDERATIONS

Audience reaction varies in different parts of the country. A society should study its local public, find out their likes and dislikes, their taste in music, in drama, in films and entertainment generally, and base its choice on what is likely to appeal to them most. This does not by any means rule out experiment and adventure in the field of new productions once a society is firmly established. On the contrary, something entirely new is often a welcome change from the round of established successes, many of which are, in any case, frequently revived by professional companies.

Having considered its public, the society must have no doubt that the choice meets with the full approval of the majority of its members. Their enthusiasm and support are essential to success, and any lack of keenness will not only reflect itself unfavourably on the production but on the sale of tickets as well.

Is the production practicable? Has the society got the players, the singers, and the right type of orchestra to do the work chosen full justice? Can it be adequately produced at reasonable cost on the stage available?

The choice of musical shows for amateur production is wide and varied. A comprehensive list of these, with the names of the copyright owners, is contained in Appendix One. It will be useful, at this stage, to consider the various types of musical shows available under their main headings: light opera, including Gilbert and Sullivan; operetta and musical comedy; the romantic musical play; revue; and pantomime.

LIGHT OPERA

Light opera, as the name suggests, calls for good singing, often at operatic level. Works like Strauss's *Die Fledermaus* and Offenbach's *The Grand Duchess* demand immaculate solo and chorus singing as well as fine orchestral playing. They should be attempted only by societies with exceptional musical talent. To do them really well is an achievement of which a society can be proud. There are many other less exacting works which come under the heading of light or comic opera which are well worth consideration, e.g. *Arlette, La Cigale, Les Cloches de Corneville, The Daughter of the Regiment, Dorothy, The Duchess of Danzig, Falka, La Fille de Madame Angot, Merrie England, Tom Jones, Monsieur Beaucaire, La Poupée, The Rebel Maid, The Rose of Persia,* and many more.

GILBERT AND SULLIVAN

The Gilbert and Sullivan operas are in a class of their own. The copyright in Sullivan's music has now expired but, fortunately, Gilbert's words remain protected until 1961.

The perfect collaboration of these two men brought something fresh and stimulating to the English musical stage at a time when its fortunes and standards were at a low ebb. Sullivan's incomparable music, wedded to Gilbert's brilliant wit, flowed like a sparkling stream through the tranquil years of late Victorian and Edwardian England.

Gilbert and Sullivan were men of the theatre. They planned their work with meticulous care, and created a tradition of comic opera peculiarly their own. Stage movements, groupings, expressions, and business were all firmly established as essential elements in the original productions. They remain so to-day. The Gilbert and Sullivan operas most frequently performed by amateur societies include *Iolanthe, Princess Ida, The Gondoliers, The Mikado, Ruddigore, The Pirates of Penzance, Patience, The Yeomen of the Guard, H.M.S. Pinafore,* and *Trial by Jury.*

OPERETTA

The operetta was originally a one-act opera, but to-day the term "operetta" is often applied to continental light operas and their English adaptations, e.g. *The Merry Widow, Gipsy Love,* etc.

Fig. 1. "The Gondoliers" (Act I): The Piazzetta, Venice
(By courtesy of Bridget D'Oyly Carte)

Fig. 2. "H.M.S. Pinafore" (Act I): Quarterdeck of H.M.S. "Pinafore" off Portsmouth

When the Viennese light operas of Franz Lehar, Oscar Straus, Leo Fall, and others were produced in England, broad comedy was introduced on the lines of the old Gaiety Theatre burlesques. This formula is also evident in the English works of Monckton, Talbot, Rubens, Caryll, and other composers and librettists. The burlesque comedy was usually written specially for famous comedians like George Graves, George Grossmith, W. H. Berry, and others, and many of the celebrated Edwardian successes owed much to these personalities.

The humour of these shows, as it appears in cold print, seems feeble and old-fashioned by present-day standards. In considering these older works on the nostalgic fame of their titles, amateurs would be wise to remember that the words, without the personalities and their "business," are liable to fall heavily on modern ears.

Many of the old favourites, however, have qualities which have survived the march of time. Several have been revised and brought up to date. The music is always memorable, and if well produced on modern standards many of these old shows still have a strong public appeal.

MUSICAL COMEDY

Musical comedy is a typically English form of entertainment, although it owes its origin to the French *opéra bouffe* in which dialogue alternates with music.

Musical comedy covers the widest range of musical shows. It allows more latitude to amateurs than light opera and musical romance. Given good singing from principals and chorus the comedy can, within reasonable limits, be brought within the scope of most capable amateur comedians by a good producer.

The older musical comedies like *Miss Hook of Holland*, *The Geisha*, *A Country Girl*, *The Arcadians*, and others have two or three full sets, while the more modern shows often run into several scenes. This change of form is probably due to the influence of American productions and to the musical film. The public became accustomed to more action, a faster *tempo*, more sophistication, and a greater variety of scene and situation. The musical comedies of the late Victorian and Edwardian years were lush, leisurely affairs, with lilting waltz

FIG. 3. "THE BALKAN PRINCESS" (ACT I): RECEPTION ROOM AT THE PALACE

From the original Prince of Wales Theatre, London, production, 1909

(By courtesy of George Dance Musical Plays)

tunes and what we regard to-day as good old-fashioned period humour, interpreted by brilliant personalities of the time.

The new phase of modern musical comedy began with *No, No, Nanette*, and has developed from this metamorphosis to the more sophisticated entertainment of to-day. This lighter type of musical show depends to a large extent on a dancing rather than a singing chorus, and on personality performances. *The Girl Friend, Please Teacher, Mr. Cinders, Yes, Madam, Mercenary Mary, Lady be Good, Jill Darling*, and many others come within this category.

The older musical comedy favourites afford considerable scope for modern interpretations so that they come fresh and new to the present generation without impairing the values which have made them endure.

THE ROMANTIC MUSICAL PLAY

The modern romantic musical play is derived from the melodrama. It contains a strong romantic plot, calls for spectacular presentation, and abounds in dramatic situations. Comedy, especially in more recent productions, occupies a secondary place in the story, while the music forms an integral part of the plot. The broad burlesque of musical comedy has been replaced by light comedy of a natural kind which is never allowed to intrude upon the plot, but is essential to it. Sometimes, as in *Carousel*, the music touches the fringe of opera.

Ivor Novello did more to foster the development of the romantic musical play than any other man of the theatre, with *Glamorous Night, Careless Rapture, Crest of the Wave, Arc de Triomphe, The Dancing Years, Perchance to Dream* and, last of all, *King's Rhapsody*.

The romantic musical play demands acting of a high order, good singing, and imaginative production. Popular spectacular shows in this category include *The Desert Song, The Student Prince, The Vagabond King, Rose Marie, The New Moon, Show Boat, Bitter Sweet*, etc.

Whichever type of work is considered—light opera, Gilbert and Sullivan, musical comedy, or romantic musical play—it should be well within the capabilities of the society. It is far wiser to do a less ambitious production really well than to

Fig. 4. "The Desert Song" (Act II, Scene 1): The Harem of Ali Ben Ali
From James Shirvell's production
(By courtesy of Samuel French, Ltd.)

attempt a spectacular show beyond the scope of the performers on an inadequate stage.

It is important when suggestions for shows are put to a vote that members realize fully what they are voting for. If possible they should be given an opportunity beforehand of reading the libretti, and examining the musical scores of the selection committee's final proposals. Failing this, a full description of the two or three shows submitted should be given before a vote is taken, and the principal numbers from the musical scores played over to the members.

REVUE

Sophisticated revue is perhaps one of the most difficult forms of entertainment for amateurs to present convincingly. Sketches and point numbers which depend largely for their successful interpretation upon star personalities should be avoided.

Amateur revue offers opportunities for local writing talent. Good-natured satire on local affairs and personalities always goes down well if cleverly written.

Amateur revue, as long as it does not attempt the impossible, makes a useful "fill-in" between musical shows for raising additional funds, and maintaining the interest of members and their public.

The essence of revue is speed and variety. Every item should be in sharp contrast to what has gone before. Light and shade should be the keynote. A quick, pointed two-minute sketch, with a punch to it, for example, can effectively follow a senti-mental number or colourful dance routine. Comedy, gay colour, rhythm; then in deep contrast a brief, tense, dramatic sketch. *Tempo* sustained all the way through. No waits, nothing too long to tire the eye or ear.

A good compère is essential but he, too, should be brief. Two pianos really well played, with drums to accentuate rhythm, can be most effective in the absence of an orchestra.

Scenery can be simple. By the use of false prosceniums, attractive drapes which take lighting well, smooth-running tabs, a few simple backcloths for sketches, groundrows for use with a cyclorama or blue skycloth for special scenes, a set of white rostrums and steps which can be moved to different

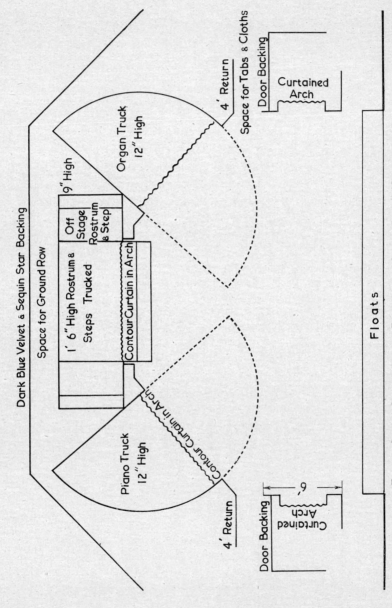

Dark Blue Velvet & Sequin Star Backing

Space for Ground Row

1' 6" High Rostrum & Steps Trucked

9" High

Off Stage Rostrum & Step

Contour Curtain in Arch

Organ Truck 12" High

4' Return

Space for Tabs & Cloths

Door Backing

Curtained Arch

Piano Truck 12" High

Contour Curtain in Arch

4' Return

Door Backing

Curtained Arch

6'

Floats

FIG. 5. SIMPLE SETTING FOR A REVUE ON A SMALL STAGE (GROUND PLAN)

A piano and organ are mounted on revolving trucks which can be swung round in front of the curtained arches for special musical items. When the trucks are returned to their former positions the forestage is left clear for sketches, etc.

Fig. 6. Simple Setting for a Revue on a Small Stage

The organ truck has been moved forward for an ensemble. The curtains in the arches can be raised or lowered, as required, and simple groundrows and backings used for a variety of scenes on the full stage.

(By courtesy of Scenic Display Services, Ltd.)

positions for a change of scene, and good lighting effects, a first-class revue can be produced at very reasonable cost.

Full use can be made of the society's chorus and dancers. A group of the best singers can be featured in songs from musical comedy and opera, subject to permission from the publishers concerned. An effective modern ballet is always popular, and full use should be made of the dancing troupe.

There is plenty of published material available for revue-sketches, concert party routines, etc., and all the music, old and new, which is likely to be required. A comprehensive selection of material from famous revues is obtainable from Samuel French, Ltd., 26 Southampton Street, Strand, London, W.C.2.

PANTOMIME

It is surprising that more amateur societies do not present pantomime as a Christmas attraction. There are, of course, difficulties in booking theatres at this time as they usually have their own pantomimes, and other accommodation is often fully booked for dances and Christmas functions. If arrangements are made well ahead, however, it is possible that suitable premises can be found.

Pantomime is a good proposition for amateurs. It occurs at the height of the festive season. Not only will it appeal to the society's regular audience, but it will attract a wider public at this time as well. It also has a strong appeal to the children.

Cinderella, perhaps the most popular of all pantomimes, and many other old favourites are available. In addition there are several charming children's plays from which to choose. Scenery, costumes, and properties present no special difficulty, but where there is no set musical score this will have to be specially arranged by the musical director.

Amateurs should not attempt to copy the professional type of pantomime. This is often designed to feature well-known variety artists and speciality acts, with the result that the story takes second place. A pantomime book which sticks to the fairy story and displays the society's talent to the best advantage should be chosen. Although it may be simpler and more modest than the spectacular professional show it will appeal just as strongly because of its originality and charm.

The audience is the final judge. It is they who have to be entertained, not the players. The choice of a musical play, or any form of musical entertainment, should be governed by the capacity of the society to do it well. A simple show, ably produced and performed, will please an audience far more than an over-ambitious choice unsuited to the abilities of the players and singers. Choose wisely, therefore, with a good margin to spare in talent and stage capacity, and public support will be deserved and won.

CHAPTER FIVE

THE PRODUCER

IT has been said that good producers are born, not made. This is only partly true. A good producer must have a natural sense of the theatre. It is this inherent faculty which enables him to appreciate, and assimilate, the technical knowledge of stagecraft and acting which in the long run are the most important qualifications of an efficient producer.

THE PRODUCER'S FUNCTION

In the field of operatic production his job is to mould many factors into a complete unity of acting, spectacle, and music. How then can an amateur hope to become an accomplished producer of musical shows? Only by intensive study, acute observation, and the exercise of a natural flair which springs from an inherent love of the theatre and an appreciation of its dramatic values.

This book is addressed to aspiring amateur producers. Professional producers have their own individual methods, derived from experience. These vary with each producer. There is no school for producers, except the school of experience. The most that can be attempted here, as far as the amateur producer is concerned, is to outline the guiding principles which will provide him with a practical groundwork for the job.

THE PROFESSIONAL PRODUCER

Professional producers are experienced men of the theatre. Very often they have been actors and stage managers before they took up production. It is not easy to find successful stage producers who will produce for amateurs as a regular calling. Because they are successful, they are often too busy for amateur work. There is, however, a certain number of highly efficient professional producers who find it worth while to produce occasionally for amateurs, but not nearly enough to go round.

There is, therefore, considerable opportunity for the amateur to apprentice himself, as it were, until he is competent to undertake production on his own account. This takes time and infinite patience.

It might be useful at this stage to consider exactly what the producer has to cope with, and to compare the average professional production with its amateur prototype.

THE PROFESSIONAL MUSICAL SHOW

What does the production of a professional musical show involve? It would not be a fair comparison to consider a new London West End production in this respect. Here, as a rule, there are the advantages of longer rehearsals on the spot, often in the theatre in which the show is being presented. Let us rather consider as a more suitable parallel the re-production of a popular musical show for tour.

The rehearsal period for a show of this nature occupies a minimum of three weeks intensive production. This has the advantage over amateur rehearsal in that it is continuous and proceeds without a break, day by day, during these weeks.

The First Week   **1118633**

During the first week, the professional cast—all accomplished artistes in the particular sphere for which they have been engaged—meet the producer on the first Monday morning to read over their parts aloud and get a rough idea of how they all fit into the show. At this first meeting the producer outlines his plan of campaign and presents his schedule for rehearsals.

It is usual to provide the leading players with full libretti in advance for preliminary study. At rehearsal all players usually work from part copies, i.e. their own dialogue with only the cues from the other characters.

Having read through the dialogue in the morning, the cast are ready the same afternoon to begin rehearsal in the form of a rough "run through" to mark entrances, exits, and main positions. That is about all the producer can hope to achieve on his first rehearsal day.

On the second day he will start building up on movements and positions. Indeed, for a few days, he will concentrate on

Fig. 7. "Madame Pompadour" (Act I): The Tavern of the "Nine Muses"
From the original Daly's Theatre, London, production, 1923
(By courtesy of Emile Littler)

FIG. 8. "VERONIQUE" (ACT III); RECEPTION ROOMS, THE TUILLERIES

(By courtesy of George Dance Musical Plays)

stage geography. Once that is more or less clear, and only then, will he attempt to tackle details of expression, characterization, and development of "business."

By the end of the first week the players will be acquainted with their lines, although they will not yet be able to rehearse without their scripts. Some actors learn their lines very quickly, others are slow to memorize them. This has nothing to do with acting ability. Very often the best actors are those who find it difficult to remember their lines in the early stages of rehearsal. The quick learner in many cases learns his lines parrot-wise without much regard for their meaning. The slower learner is probably studying and analysing as he goes along, and the values he is building up will not become apparent until later in rehearsal.

In the course of the first week a pianist will be available to play over the principals' numbers. These will be rehearsed to break everyone in and give the players, and the producer, an overall idea of the musical side of the show as far as the principal parts are concerned. The principals will probably have had an opportunity of studying and practising their musical numbers before rehearsals are called; if that is so, too much time need not be devoted to the preliminary run through.

Rehearsals run daily, as a rule, from 10 a.m. to 6 p.m., or seven hours a day, allowing for a lunch break. In addition, singing principals may rehearse on some evenings with their coaches for an hour or so after the daily rehearsal. Thus, during the first week the principals, concentrating on the dialogue, with a brief introduction to the singing, rehearse for a minimum of forty-two hours, plus extra coaching and study at home.

The Second Week

During the second week, three rehearsals will be taking place simultaneously—dialogue, singing, and dancing. The producer can now concentrate on the development of situations, dialogue interpretation, expression, and polishing up the musical side.

At the same time, during the second week, the chorus will be rehearsing elsewhere under the musical director or chorus master. The dancers will also be rehearsing separately under the dance producer or ballet mistress in close consultation with the producer.

During this week some time will be allowed each day so that the principals can join the chorus for an hour's singing rehearsal of the ensembles, finales, and other chorus numbers in which principals are concerned. Similarly, the dancers, who may be expected to sing in certain ensembles and finales, will be given a break from their dance routines to rehearse with the chorus. During the week principals will be released from dialogue rehearsals as convenient so that they can rehearse their dance routines with the dance producer.

Thus, during the second week, the chorus will have put in forty-two hours rehearsal, the dancers approximately the same, and the principals a further forty-two hours plus coaching and extra rehearsals in the evening for dialogue, dancing, and singing, as the producer may direct.

The Third Week

During the third week the entire company will rehearse together. By this time the producer will have worked up dialogue and action to the point at which he can go right ahead with the show as a whole without undue interruption. He will also spend time on the more difficult scenes and ensembles in conjunction with the dance producer, but he will aim at running through the entire show, act by act, at least once every day.

These final rehearsals take place in a large hall or on a theatre stage. No time is wasted. A small room is usually set aside so that principals can go on with their dialogue and music rehearsals, polishing up action and timing, when they are not required for the general rehearsal. The dancers, too, continue their routines quietly at the end of the hall, in another part of the theatre or in a separate room, when they are not needed in the ensembles, etc.

During the three weeks of rehearsal, the cast visit the costumiers to have their costumes fitted, and a dress parade is usually held on the Friday morning of the third week for a final check-up. On Friday afternoon, the producer will run the show right through for the last time prior to the dress rehearsal without a break so that it can be timed accurately. Any serious faults will be corrected at a late rehearsal on Friday evening.

As the company will be travelling on Sunday to the town in which they open with the show, there is usually no rehearsal on the Saturday.

On the Sunday, the scenery is set up, positions marked, and changes rehearsed. Properties, furniture, and costumes are carefully checked. The dress rehearsal begins as soon as the stage director reports everything clear.

A band call, which the entire company attend for music rehearsal with the orchestra, is held on the Monday morning. Lighting details are completed during the comparative peace of the afternoon. A last-minute recapitulation by the producer of outstanding dress rehearsal faults, and the curtain rises on the first performance.

During three weeks of *continuous* rehearsal, principals will have worked for a minimum of 119 hours; chorus and dancers 77 hours, excluding the dress rehearsal.

THE AMATEUR PRODUCER

The professional producer has the advantage of experienced actors, singers, dancers, technicians, and musicians, while the producer of amateur shows has to work mainly with comparatively inexperienced material. In a professional production there is continuity of rehearsal; amateur rehearsals are intermittent and spread over a longer period of time.

To get the best out of the material at his disposal, the amateur producer must employ considerable tact, display infinite patience, and be able to exercise authority and discipline. His amateur players are not being paid for their services, so that he can maintain discipline only by means of a persuasive personality, a firmness of purpose, and a knowledge of his job. Once he can convince his cast that he not only knows what he wants, but also knows how to get it, they will respond with loyal and keen support.

In order to qualify as a producer, the amateur should study the professional producer's methods. He can do this at rehearsals and by watching professional productions in the theatre. He should get in touch with his local theatre and learn all he can about stage routine and equipment. After a while, he should volunteer for stage management in his amateur society—the quickest way of gaining practical experience.

Fig. 9. "A Waltz Dream" (Act I): Festival Hall in Prince Joachim's Castle in Flauserthurn

From James Shirvell's production

(By courtesy of George Dance Musical Plays)

If the opportunity of producing a straight play, i.e. a non-musical play, presents itself he should take it. It is useful experience and will give him the confidence and authority which he will require for the more complex job of directing a musical production.

CHAPTER SIX

PRODUCTION

No producer can begin his work without a cast, and the success of a musical show depends a great deal upon careful casting.

CASTING

Any suggestion of favouritism in allocating parts, or a feeling among members that the casting is permanently in the hands of a small "clique," can cause much resentment and dissatisfaction. Casting should be scrupulously impartial, based entirely on merit and suitability for the part, and on nothing else.

The selection committee entrusted with this delicate task should be freely elected by a majority vote of all members. Every opportunity should be given to new talent. The tendency among some amateur societies to favour influential members, irrespective of merit, by giving them leading parts in every show, is fortunately on the decline.

The available parts are, of course, few in relation to the number of aspiring members, but if the casting is conducted with patience and consideration in an atmosphere of fairness and impartiality, the first disappointments will soon be forgotten, and enthusiasm restored once rehearsals begin.

The producer, musical director, and dance producer should all be present, if possible, at the audition for parts. The producer will have all the characters in the show clearly in his mind, and his recommendations should have prior consideration. The musical director and dance producer, too, will offer expert advice on their side of the production.

The producer's views on the cast are most important. After all, he has to produce the show, and probably knows more about it than anyone else present. Because of his experience and close study of the show in all its details, he can often pick out, at an audition, potential talent which may not be immediately apparent to many members of the casting committee.

Only on rare occasions can the perfect cast be realized. The best that can be done is to get as near the ideal as possible. The important thing is to secure a proper balance among the characters. Personalities for different roles should not be too similar in type; contrast in types gives light and shade to the production. The stout comedienne often pairs off best with the small comedian, and vice versa. On the other hand, a short portly tenor, playing opposite a tall soprano in the leading romantic parts can often be funnier than the comedians.

Sometimes a part can be modified slightly to suit the personality of a player who may not conform physically with the conventional conception of the part, but otherwise fulfils all the requirements. It may, for example, be a comedy role originally played on the professional stage by a big man. This may not be important, although it may be suggested in the libretto. The part may have been adapted in the first instance to suit a professional star player who happened to be big, and there is no reason why minor alterations should not be made to suit a small man if he is a good comedian.

A decision has often to be made between Miss X who can make a first-class job of the singing but is not a very good actress, and Miss Y who is an excellent actress but rather shaky on her top notes. The choice depends entirely on the nature of the show. If it is a light opera which demands, above all else, immaculate singing, Miss X is the obvious choice. If on the other hand it is a musical play, or musical comedy, in which acting and personality predominate, then it should be Miss Y. Miss X will naturally be disappointed, but the show will benefit.

In the lighter type of musical comedy, charm, youth, and dancing efficiency often mean more than good singing voices. Unless a society can cast players of this calibre it is wiser to leave this kind of show alone.

The casting of small parts and understudies should be done with as much care as the leading roles. Minor parts are too often rushed through at auditions or left over until late in the rehearsal period. A show can be marred by indifferent small-part casting. Consider how well small parts are played in films and on the professional stage. Many an actor has made a name for himself by a brilliant character study in a tiny part.

A large number of aspirants will present themselves at auditions for leading parts. The majority will have neither the

Fig. 10. "The Maid of the Mountains" (Act II): Courtyard of the Governor's Palace
Emile Littler's London Coliseum production, 1942

voices nor the acting ability to fulfil their ambitions. Some will
be nervous and self-conscious, for which due allowance should
be made. A word of encouragement goes a long way and a
period of apprenticeship in the chorus will give them confidence.

PLANNING REHEARSALS

The producer should make out a detailed schedule covering the
number of rehearsal hours available during the rehearsal weeks.

He should plan every detail of the production beforehand.
Some producers use model stages to work out movements and
groupings. This is a very good idea if time can be found to do
it properly. It means making model reproductions of the sets
of scenery to scale, and small cut-out figures to represent the
cast and chorus. A simple alternative is to use small pieces of
thin cardboard—old visiting cards cut up will do—representing
the characters. These little squares are marked up with
abbreviations of the characters' names. The various movements are worked out on a small table, from the libretto. All
the entrances, exits, and groupings, as well as the movements
in the action can thus be worked out like a game of chess, and
entered in the producer's working script before rehearsals begin.
This is much more satisfactory than trying to "work off the
cuff" at rehearsal, on the trial and error method, which usually
ends in confusing the cast and the producer as well.

The principals should be urged to learn their lines as soon as
possible so that the producer can begin building up expression
and situations. Until the cast do know their lines the producer
should go easy during the early rehearsals. If he tries to do too
much at first, he will find his efforts wasted. Until the cast
at least know what they are talking about, i.e. know the *meaning*
of their lines, production in detail will only confuse them.

During the first phase of principals' rehearsals the chorus and
dancers should, if possible, be rehearsing elsewhere. If circumstances permit, the rehearsal rooms should be in the same
building so that the producer can exercise control over all the
proceedings. The largest room, in which the full company will
rehearse together, should be at least the same size as the stage
on which the show will take place.

When the company are ready to rehearse together the producer should arrange his rehearsals so that, as far as possible,

members of the cast are not left with nothing to do for long periods. If this problem is not dealt with, interest will wane and discipline slacken. If it is possible to arrange for two or three rehearsal rooms, however, all three elements in the show—principals, chorus, and dancers—can be kept occupied and interested all the time. It will also save much valuable time, as well as keeping everyone on their toes, in more ways than one.

It is useful if sketches or photographs of the scenes in the show can be permanently on view in the main rehearsal room. In spite of the most painstaking explanation by the producer, it is surprising how confused many members of the company can be, even at the dress rehearsal, about their entrances and exits and the geography of the sets generally.

THE REHEARSAL SCHEDULE

How long should an amateur operatic company rehearse? How many rehearsals are required? What matters most, of course, is the total number of rehearsal *hours* available.

The impresarios who put on professional musical shows are not philanthropists, but shrewd business men of the theatre. They have, through long experience, arrived at a rehearsal schedule which, with professional artistes, represents the *minimum* time required to ensure a polished production on the opening night. We have seen, in the previous chapter, that not less than three weeks of continuous rehearsal are necessary to produce a professional musical show for tour, as distinct from a new West End production, which may occupy as long as six or even eight weeks.

On a three weeks basis the total number of rehearsal hours work out as follows—

	hours
First Week—	
Principals only	42
Second Week—Separate Rehearsals—	
Principals	42
Chorus	42
Dancers	42
Third Week—Combined Rehearsals—	
Full Company (5 days)	35
TOTALS—	
Principals	119
Chorus	77
Dancers	77

The above schedule does not include extra evening or Sunday rehearsals which the producer may find it necessay to call. Nor does it allow for coaching rehearsals privately arranged by principals. The schedule may vary, of course, according to the nature of the production. It may be necessary, for example, to extend chorus rehearsals if the concerted work is unusually difficult.

During the first two weeks the preparatory work has been fully covered, and progress during the third week will therefore be rapid. It is during this week that the three carefully rehearsed elements—acting, singing, and dancing—are co-ordinated by the producer.

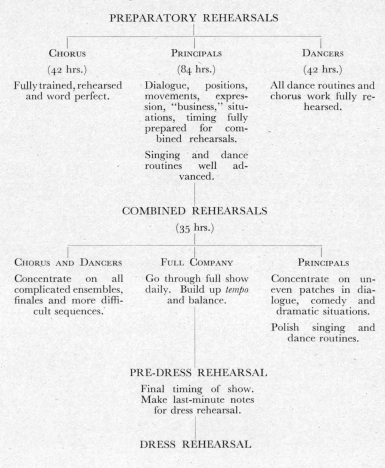

PREPARATORY REHEARSALS

CHORUS	PRINCIPALS	DANCERS
(42 hrs.)	(84 hrs.)	(42 hrs.)
Fully trained, rehearsed and word perfect.	Dialogue, positions, movements, expression, "business," situations, timing fully prepared for combined rehearsals. Singing and dance routines well advanced.	All dance routines and chorus work fully rehearsed.

COMBINED REHEARSALS

(35 hrs.)

CHORUS AND DANCERS	FULL COMPANY	PRINCIPALS
Concentrate on all complicated ensembles, finales and more difficult sequences.	Go through full show daily. Build up *tempo* and balance.	Concentrate on uneven patches in dialogue, comedy and dramatic situations. Polish singing and dance routines.

PRE-DRESS REHEARSAL

Final timing of show. Make last-minute notes for dress rehearsal.

DRESS REHEARSAL

The producer of an amateur show should try to get as near the professional schedule in rehearsal time as possible. As his rehearsals are not consecutive and his players are amateurs, he will need all the time at his disposal. However long this may be, much time can be saved by adequate preparatory rehearsal before combined rehearsals with the full company begin. When they do, he will be better able to concentrate on giving the production pace, personality, and shape.

THE FIRST READING

At the first principals' rehearsal, the producer should outline his plans, and explain his rehearsal schedule. He should urge upon all the necessity for immediate study, so that he can get down to the real work of production at the earliest possible moment. He can really do little in the way of detail work until they get rid of their books.

Having briefly outlined the theme of the show, the producer should indicate how he proposes to deal with the production. It is important for him to impress upon everyone that he has a clear-cut idea of what he is going to do, and how he is going to do it.

The cast should then read the libretto aloud. This enables the players to obtain a comprehensive idea of the plot by hearing the lines spoken. It also gives the producer an idea how his cast are going to shape, and their suitability for the parts allotted to them. He can also indicate briefly in the course of the reading any serious faults in each reader's interpretation of a part, and correct them.

The proper pronunciation of character and place names should be settled at the reading and also the question of accents and foreign words. Many amateurs are inclined to overdo foreign accents and dialects, often to such an extent that the audience have difficulty in following what they are saying. Some dialects are more difficult to reproduce than others, and it is often better for amateurs to concentrate on the general characteristics and rhythm of a language or dialect, emphasizing only the more obvious words, than to attempt a detailed interpretation without a very complete study of the subject.

After the reading, the producer should invite discussion on the various parts so that any doubts and ambiguities on general interpretation are cleared up before actual rehearsals begin.

The production value of a musical show depends upon the capacity of the producer to co-ordinate successfully the three elements of dialogue, singing, and choreography. The sooner he can get busy on this the better. He can do so only when the principals, chorus, and dancers know their lines, their music, and their dance routines.

THE PRINCIPALS' REHEARSALS

The principals should be urged to learn their dialogue immediately, and to study their parts and the *meaning* of their lines at every available opportunity. Unless they are working from part copies, they should be encouraged to mark their parts in the libretto so that they can find their places quickly on their cues. There is nothing more irritating to a producer than to have the flow of dialogue held up by a player fumbling through the pages of his script to find his place. It is often a good plan for the cast to copy out their lines, with the cues, into small note-books which they can conveniently turn to for study in their spare time, as well as at rehearsal. The act of copying, too, is an aid to memory.

The producer should not try to achieve too much in the early stages of rehearsal. He should concentrate first on positions and general interpretation, rather than on detail which the principals can absorb only when they are familiar with their lines.

The stage manager should be present at rehearsals and it is his responsibility to enter in the prompt copy all stage entrances, exits, movements, and dialogue which the producer may have altered or added to the libretto. The principals, and the producer, should also record these changes in their copies so that confusion and argument about what was decided at preceding rehearsals will be avoided.

Punctuality at all rehearsals should be insisted upon, but the producer should call principals only when they are actually required, unless, of course, they wish to be present to watch. He should tell them at the end of each rehearsal what he proposes to do in the next, so that they know exactly when they will be required.

It is advisable to arrange the first dialogue rehearsals on consecutive days so that the cast may get to know their entrances, exits, and main positions at the earliest possible moment.

Before rehearsals start, the producer and stage manager should set the stage. It is the stage manager's job to do this at subsequent rehearsals.

A space on the floor equal to the acting area of the stage on which the production will take place should be marked off at each corner with chalk. The positions of entrances, doors, exits, staircases, rostrums and other items should also be marked, and the geography of the scene explained to the cast in conjunction with the drawings or photographs displayed in the rehearsal room. Chairs, tables, stools, etc., should be used to represent as far as possible the furniture and other objects in the actual scene.

Properties should be used at all rehearsals. If certain items are not available something should be provided to represent them. Hats, coats, cloaks, walking sticks, umbrellas, parasols, trays, glasses, cups and saucers, and other properties should always be represented at rehearsal so that players who have to use them in the show can learn to manipulate them easily and naturally.

Understudies should be encouraged to attend dialogue rehearsals if they are not fully occupied with chorus rehearsing. They should be provided with parts and not made to feel that they are unimportant. They should study their parts as carefully as the principals, and rehearse them in the unavoidable absence of any player.

All stage directions given by the producer are from the actor's viewpoint. Thus the instruction in the libretto "Enter HARRY L." refers to *Harry's* left.

Home study by principals is important, especially during the early rehearsal period. The various points which have been brought out at rehearsal should be gone over again and again in private by each member of the cast.

The opening and closing of doors, wearing and carrying properties, and so on, should be diligently practised at home until they all come smoothly and naturally. Expression and deportment should be rehearsed in front of a mirror. Lines should be repeated until the proper inflexions recommended by the producer are perfected. In doing all this, amateurs are, in fact, going through a very necessary course of self-training which, in some measure, will compensate for their lack of professional technique.

GETTING THE BEST OUT OF THE CAST

Professional players are paid for their work. They are cast for their parts because they are competent artistes and will do what an efficient producer tells them without question once he has gained their confidence. They will turn up punctually for all rehearsals as requested, and are more subject to discipline and control than amateur players. If not, they will be quickly replaced by others.

In dealing with amateurs, the producer has to approach his task from a different angle. They are not paid for their work, and the producer has therefore to rely entirely upon their enthusiasm and interest for his results. He must, through his own enthusiasm and personality, carry them along with him so that with every rehearsal they will feel that they are being guided by an experienced hand, progressively and surely towards the most effective interpretation of their roles.

Because they are amateurs, the producer will have more to teach them. He will have to show many of them how to make an entrance and an exit properly; how to move naturally about the stage; what to do and what not to do with their hands. He will have to teach them the art of listening, of standing and sitting still; the art of timing; how to speak clearly and effectively; how to make the most of their singing and dancing; and a dozen other things the professional does as a matter of course because of his training and experience in a full-time job.

To get the best work out of his amateur team the producer has to be a good psychologist. He will have to study his players and deal with each of them in a slightly different way according to their nature and personality. He will find vanity, self-consciousness, lack of control, nervousness, apparent stupidity, over-confidence, inability to concentrate, and sometimes antipathy—all of which he will have to break down and master. He must never attempt to do this by bullying and bravado. That is the quickest way to failure. Good producers seldom shout, even when their patience is tried to the limit, as it often

FIG. 11. "DEAR MISS PHOEBE" (ACT II) : THE WATERLOO BALL
From the original Phoenix Theatre, London, production, 1950
(By courtesy of Emile Littler)

is. Nor will any good come from sarcasm or by making a player look foolish in front of the cast. That is the way to lose members for the society. If a player is temperamentally difficult, or is not responding sufficiently to direction, the best way is to take him or her aside from the others and discuss the situation in a quiet, persuasive, sympathetic manner, explaining where the fault lies, and how to correct it.

A celebrated and rather conceited stage actor once accepted a small but important part in a film. The film director, a shrewd psychologist, appreciated that as it was the actor's first film, a certain amount of tact would be required to avoid any suggestion that the great man might have to be told how to act in front of the camera. A scene was duly rehearsed. The result, for film purposes, was terrible, but the director did not say so. Instead, he congratulated the actor on an excellent performance, but suggested casually that the scene might be slightly improved if one of the lines were said a little differently, and a certain movement modified to suit the camera angle. The actor swelled with pride and the scene was rehearsed again. Once more the director enthused at the result, which was now a little better. In the end the scene was rehearsed ten times before it was shot. Each time the same tactful approach was made. Each time the director introduced little changes, always accompanied by praise and encouragement, until the scene was done exactly the way *he* wanted it. The actor grew more and more interested with each attempt, more convinced that he was brilliant in the scene and that the director knew it.

The director got his way. He knew his man. Had he been impatient or tactless, the actor would probably have walked out of the studio. Which goes to prove that a good producer, like a good film director, will get the best work out of his team by encouragement and a sympathetic understanding of their various personalities.

CHAPTER SEVEN

THE PRODUCER AND THE ACTOR

STAGE dialogue is not necessarily natural everyday speech. It should *sound* like it. Good dialogue is contrived to motivate the plot, progress the action, and develop character and situations. While dialogue must sound natural, it must also be informative so that the audience can readily understand the progress of the plot.

CLARITY OF SPEECH

Clarity of speech is a first essential. Nothing is more irritating to an audience than inaudibility. It should be impressed upon all players with lines to speak—or sing—that they have to be distinctly heard in *every* part of the theatre, in the back row of the gallery or circle, as well as in the front row of the stalls. It is not enough to speak as in ordinary conversation. The voice must be projected, from the lungs, to produce the timbre and resonance necessary to carry it across the footlights without shouting.

Words should be clearly enunciated, but not over-enunciated so that the dialogue in its style of delivery smacks of the elocution class. Constant practice in reading lines aloud, and listening to well-spoken dialogue in the theatre, in the cinema, on the radio, and on television, all provide useful groundwork for developing voice production and clarity of diction. It is not the producer's function to teach his players voice production, breath control, and how to speak the Queen's English properly. He can only give useful hints on how the particular dialogue for a part can be most effectively expressed. The best plan is to seek a first-class modern teacher, avoiding the old-fashioned elocution class like the plague.

EXPRESSION

Without adequate expression, clearly enunciated words would be dull and meaningless. Unless a player thoroughly understands

the *meaning* of the lines he is speaking, and their signifi-
cance to the plot and other characters, they will lack conviction. The emphasis of essential words gives dialogue value
and meaning. Effective speech demands light and shade, and
a rhythmic quality, to make it sound interesting to an audience.

TIMING

Timing is most important. If what has to be said by a player
is not said at the exact second, and with the correct emphasis,
the words will lose half their meaning. A dramatic scene,
working up to a climax of action, calls for exciting and inspired
dialogue which should make the audience tense with anticipation. In this case the timing will make for speed in taking up
cues and a quickening of speech, which, in conjunction with the
expression put into the lines, will suggest mounting tension.
There may, however, be a vital line of dialogue before the
climax which is so unexpected and dramatic in its impact that
it calls for a significant pause before it is spoken. This pause
will heighten the tension, and the whole effect will be lost if the
producer fails to appreciate its value.

DEVELOPING THE ACTOR'S PERSONALITY

One of the producer's tasks is to develop the personality of his
players, both vocally and visually—vocal personality to
present in the most effective way what each character should
sound like, and visual personality to convey what each character
should *look* and act like. And this applies to chorus and small
parts as much as to principals.

It should be impressed on the cast that they have to convey
this vocal and visual interpretation of character and scene to
their audience from a distance. The orchestra pit separates
them from the stalls, and the vast space of the auditorium from
the heights of the gallery and circles. To speak and act as
they do in everyday life will not come across effectively to the
audience on the other side of the footlights. In a small hall
the same applies, although to a lesser degree. It is important,
therefore, that the producer should know his stage and auditorium thoroughly so that he can set action and expression at
the correct pitch according to the conditions. In films, the
opposite is the case. Stage actors have to be more restrained

in their actions and speech on film because their every expression, visual and vocal, is subjected to the magnification of the camera lens, the use of the close-up, and the sensitivity of the microphone. Their voices on the screen are amplified by mechanical means so that the faintest whisper can be heard in every part of the auditorium. On the stage, the actor has to rely entirely on his own technique to project his art across the footlights. By experience he grows to *feel* the effect his words and actions are having on the audience in the course of every performance. He will adjust his technique, his interpretation, and his timing to a fine degree until he is in perfect tune with his audience. One has only to compare the timing and technique of a comedian working to a small diffident audience on a Monday night with his *tempo* and method of attack on a Saturday night, inspired by a crowded, responsive house. The audience is part of the show, and he adjusts his *tempo* to their reaction. The same applies in varying degrees to all forms of stage interpretation. In drama, the actor will feel the effect his art is having on his audience just as much as the comedian exploiting his laughs.

GAINING CONFIDENCE

In dramatic and love scenes some amateur actors are inclined to feel self-conscious. This is largely due to the fear that they may look foolish to their friends in the audience. The producer must impress upon his cast that sincerity is essential to effective dramatic acting. He can soon get rid of self-consciousness in his players by a few simple, precise instructions on speech and movements once they know their lines. If they are assured that there is nothing to worry about in a difficult scene they will gain confidence with every rehearsal. Once their inferiority complex has been overcome, the producer can develop the scene gradually in more detail until it is perfect. It is worth while spending some extra time on scenes of this kind. When they are well done they can make all the difference to a show.

Many amateurs do not know what to do with their hands on the stage. The short answer is nothing, preferably, until the producer tells them. They must learn the art of standing still. They must be taught not to clutch the furniture, nor keep putting their hands in their pockets, and other forms of nervous restlessness which only serve to distract the audience.

It should be appreciated that dialogue consists of people talking to each other. While some talk, others listen, and those who listen should be as attentive to what is being said to them as the audience. Repose when repose is necessary.

Personality and charm will compensate for many short-comings in amateur acting. These virtues should be encouraged and exploited by the producer.

To become a good actor, the amateur must be intelligent and observant. The producer can guide him technically but the ability to *create* a part must come from within. It is from his experience of life, his imagination, and his observation of character that the actor must find inspiration. The little touches of expression, the typical mannerisms which emerge from a knowledge and study of human nature, bring richness and colour to the interpretation of character. Given these qualities, even in small measure, the amateur actor will respond more readily to the expert guidance and wider technical experience of the producer.

ACTION AND MOVEMENT

As with dialogue, timing is equally important in action and movement. Production technique has advanced over the years since the early musical comedies. The *tempo* of life has quickened. Audiences are harder to please. They expect more action and speed in their entertainment. The amateur producer should bear this in mind when dealing with older works. Dance routines and chorus work must be speeded up, out-dated dialogue and "business" modernized, and new methods applied to give the old masters new life. Even if the plot is not all it should be, speed and an atmosphere of gaiety and excitement can be injected into a show by skilful pro-duction.

Entrances should be taken up quickly on the cues. Princi-pals' entrances and exits should be thoroughly rehearsed, time and again, until they are perfect in timing and movement. Too often they are scamped at rehearsal owing to lack of space.

Exit lines should be given due attention. They have usually been written for effect, and the way in which they are delivered

Fig. 12. Ensemble from Act I, Scene 2 of "The Song of Norway": A Square on the Outskirts of Bergen

From the Palace Theatre, London, production, 1946

(By courtesy of Emile Littler)

and the action which goes with them should be carefully rehearsed.

The actor should avoid giving the impression, in making his exit, that he is retiring to the wings to do his football pools. Some actors—and this is not confined to amateurs by any means—stop acting before they leave the stage, thus destroying the illusion of the scene. Both in entering and on making an exit, a player should begin to act *before* he comes on and continue to act until his exit is complete and he is out of sight of the audience.

A good actor will convey the right atmosphere of the play in the manner of his entrance. He will vary this according to whether he is supposed, for example, to have entered from the next room, the house next door, after a short train journey, or from the other side of the world.

In exterior scenes, entrances and exits should produce the impression that the landscape does extend beyond the limits of the stage and that the players, when they enter, have come from somewhere, and on their exit, are going somewhere related to the locale of the scene.

Principals should be so directed as not to leave the centre area of the stage empty for any length of time. On the other hand, action should not be monotonously confined to dead stage centre. The best positioning depends largely on the setting and the situations, but the audience's line of sight from various parts of the auditorium should not be forgotten. Action should be set far enough in on either side of the stage to ensure that it is not cut off from view at the sides of the stalls, and far enough down stage so that it is in sight of the audience at the back of the circle or gallery. This has to be watched particularly when high rostrums, staircases, or truck sets with second-floor structures are used. The height of borders is also important here.

CHORUS PRODUCTION

Chorus entrances should be carefully rehearsed in detail. A common production fault is the sudden, untidy entrance of the chorus on the cue for an ensemble or finale. They come wandering on from the wings for no apparent reason except "cue for song." The audience, however, have anticipated their

Fig. 13. Ensemble from Scene 5 of "Annie Get Your Gun"
From the original London Coliseum production, 1947
(By courtesy of Emile Littler)

entrance by watching their shadows on the backcloth or wings for some time during the scene. This is bad production. The chorus should be properly rehearsed to make an effective entrance for some logical reason. The movement of every individual should be worked out so that the entrance, according to the situation, is animated, colourful, and orderly. They should each be given specific movements by the producer and, if applicable, short lines of dialogue to produce the effect of a general "buzz" of conversation and bring them smoothly and naturally into their positions for the ensemble.

The production of ensembles and chorus movements is frequently the sole province of the dance producer, but the producer himself should indicate the broad effects he requires. The dance producer, or ballet mistress, can then base the routines of dancing and movement on the producer's general ideas which have regard for the overall effect and balance of the show as a whole. The producer and dance producer should, in fact, work in the closest consultation with each other in all these matters. The tendency with some producers to leave everything to the dance producer often results in a patchy, unbalanced production which never comes to life as a co-ordinated and imaginative piece of work.

The chorus are often inclined to crowd the centre of the stage, leaving gaps at the sides. This is frequently due to insufficient space at rehearsals, and it is difficult to break them of the habit unless it is pointed out to them at the beginning, when their positions should be set exactly and maintained at all rehearsals.

Chorus reaction to dialogue is another rehearsal point which does not always receive sufficient attention. When a comedy line, for example, calls for laughter from the chorus it should be definite and sustained, and not, as is often the case, insincere, half-hearted, and entirely unnatural. The joke the comedian has made may be as old as Time, but it may sound reasonably funny to the audience if sixty people on the stage react to it with robust, convincing laughter.

The same applies to cheering crowds, and to scenes suggesting excitement and drama. Time spent on working these supporting effects up to the highest pitch of realism is well worth while.

The chorus should be trained at rehearsal to keep spaces clear for principals' entrances and exits. Here again there is a tendency for some members of the chorus to move from the positions the producer has given them, and bunch themselves right in the path of some unfortunate player who has to battle his way through them to get to the centre of the stage. This irritating fault is often due to a lack of interest on the part of the miscreants in the action of the play and an ignorance of the geography of the scene.

Faults like these can be most effectively corrected by appointing a head girl in charge of the female chorus, and a head man to look after the male section. These members become responsible for discipline generally among the chorus, and can be of great assistance to the producer in seeing that the various rehearsal points are strictly observed.

It is a curious fact that while at times the producer has difficulty in getting the chorus to make enough noise, he often finds more difficulty in commanding silence and absolute stillness on the stage when it is most required. A tense climax, with everyone on the stage, can be ruined even by some slight movement or noise. In this case the situation should be briefly explained to the cast so that everyone understands its dramatic impact. The chorus are there not only to sing but to act, and their co-operation can be more easily obtained if they are told as much as possible about the plot and the situations.

CHAPTER EIGHT

THE MUSICAL DIRECTOR

THE qualities most desirable in a theatrical conductor may be summarized as follows—

1. The ability to read music at sight, and to play the Piano (the former essential, the latter not absolutely so, but very desirable).

2. Some acquaintance with the instruments of the orchestra, and the principles of harmony, composition, orchestration, and vocal technique.

3. A thorough knowledge of the technique of conducting, a sensitive ear, and a sense of the theatre.

4. Self-confidence, imagination, tact, and a strong sense of discipline.

THE SELECTION OF A MUSICAL DIRECTOR

This formidable array of attributes is generally to be found together only in the professional musician of wide experience, and amateur societies are not always in a position to secure the services of such a musical director. The choice of a conductor must then be made from those amateur musicians who are immediately available. This is a choice not to be made lightly. The musical directorship of a society is a responsible position, and there may be several aspiring amateurs only too eager to accept it. If, however, someone with local connexions is appointed, and he subsequently proves himself unsuited to the task, it may be difficult to avoid bad feeling when it becomes necessary to replace him by a more competent conductor.

If there is no one available with previous experience of theatrical conducting, an organist and choirmaster may possibly be the best choice, since his work should enable him to take the training of the chorus and principals in his stride, even if his knowledge of the orchestra is somewhat limited. Many such organists are able to direct performances of the Gilbert and Sullivan operas (and similar works) very

64

competently, though they are often less successful with musical comedies such as *No, No, Nanette*, where speed and lightness of touch are even more essential than accurate chorus singing. In a fast-moving show, the ability to pick up cues smartly, and to keep the music flowing throughout, is of paramount importance.

If, on the other hand, a competent conductor is available who is accustomed to handling an orchestra, but is less experienced in choral work, it is often possible for the preliminary work of training the chorus and principals to be undertaken by a chorus master.

RELATIONS BETWEEN PRODUCER AND MUSICAL DIRECTOR

In order that production arrangements may be smoothly carried out, complete understanding should exist between the producer and the musical director. The feeling that either is interfering in matters which do not concern him is bound to lead to bad relations which may seriously affect the success of the production. To guard against any such unfortunate situation, a working agreement should be established, so that the musical director will have the final word in all purely musical matters, but will defer to the producer whenever the music is related to dramatic action.

THE TECHNIQUE OF CONDUCTING

Stick or no Stick?

There is no reason why a conductor should use a stick if he finds that he can secure satisfactory results without one. Each method has something in its favour; the hand alone is more expressive than a piece of wood, while a beat given with a stick is more precise, and can be better seen by the performers. It is also less tiring to use a stick, especially when beating quickly.

Choosing the Stick

Sticks vary considerably in length, weight, and thickness, and pains should be taken to choose one which will give the maximum of control with the minimum of effort. The stick should be light in weight and colour (it is often painted white so that it may be easily seen), and the cramped conditions of some orchestra pits make it advisable that it should be not more than eighteen inches in length. A stick with a wooden bulb or a cork handle at the lower end is less likely to slip out of the fingers, or cause hand and finger cramp, than a plain stick.

Holding the Stick

The stick, which should be imagined as an extension of the hand, should be lightly but firmly held between the thumb and the first and second fingers of the right hand,[1] the other fingers being either left free or lightly closed around the stick. The size of the beat is varied according to the loudness or softness of the music; in quiet passages the beat will come from the fingers and wrist alone, in moderately loud passages from the forearm moving from the elbow, and in a *fortissimo* from the whole arm moving from the shoulder. The wrist, elbow, and shoulder joints must remain loose and flexible throughout.

The Starting Position

Before beginning to conduct a musical number, the stick should be raised to the starting position, and held there for a few seconds in order to prepare the orchestra for the start. In this position the stick should be about level with the chest and should point upwards and inwards, and the elbow should be kept well away from the body.

The conductor must stand sufficiently high, so that the stick can be seen clearly by every member of the orchestra. If he finds that some players cannot see the stick, he should have the conductor's rostrum made higher; it is tiring to conduct for any length of time with the arms raised above the normal level.

When assuming the starting position the conductor should remain quite still, quietly looking to see that he has the attention of his players, and that they are ready to begin.

Beating Time

The conductor's first duty is to give a clear and precise beat. The essential movements in beating time are comparatively

---

[1] There is no reason why left-handed conductors should not hold the stick in the left hand.

simple, but a decisive beat is only to be acquired by continued practice. Normally the right hand gives the beat, and the left hand signals entries to singers and players, and indicates expression. This does not mean that the right hand should be regarded merely as a kind of metronome; the movements of the stick, while leaving the performers in no doubt as to the position of each beat, should also express the character of the music (phrasing, degree of loudness or softness, *legato* or *staccato*, etc.).

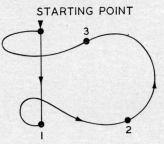

FIG. 14. TRIPLE TIME

Normally, music has either two, three, or four beats in a bar. In conducting, the first beat, which receives the strongest accent, is always indicated by a downward movement of the stick, and the last beat by an upward movement. The second of three beats is shown by a movement to the right; and the second and third of four beats by movements to the left and right. Thus the directions in which the stick moves are as follows—

2 BEATS IN A BAR (DUPLE TIME)
1. Down.   2. Up.

3 BEATS IN A BAR (TRIPLE TIME)
1. Down.   2. Right.   3. Up.

4 BEATS IN A BAR (QUADRUPLE TIME)
1. Down.   2. Left.   3. Right.   4. Up.

FIG. 15. TRIPLE TIME

We have now to consider the fundamental principles of time beating.

(*a*) Except for the down beat (which may be represented as a straight line) the stick must move from one point to another in a curve. In Triple Time, for example, the stick should move roughly as shown in Fig. 14.

If the stick were moved in a straight line from point to point, as in Fig. 15, it would be impossible for the performers to judge exactly where one beat ended and the next was due to begin.

The diagrams usually included in books on conducting give

only a general idea of the movements of the stick; the actions of a conductor's hand are too complex to be followed minutely from a diagram.

(b) Fig. 14 shows three black dots. At each of these points the stick is arrested momentarily by a slight action of the wrist which causes a bounce, usually described (in books on conducting) as a "click." The click marks the exact point at which each beat *begins*,[1] and enables the performers to judge the duration of each beat (the interval between two clicks). After the stick has clicked on the beat the hand immediately moves on, gradually gathering speed until it is slowed down by the next click. To some extent, the click is present in every beat (except where there is a sustained chord, or a rest), but it varies in form from a definite bounce to a slight movement of the fingers, according to whether the music is *staccato* or *legato*. The click should be thought of not as a stopping place, but as an elastic point at which the stick is deflected towards the next point; except when there is a pause in the music, the stick must always be kept moving.

Subdividing the Beat

The beats in a bar of music—two, three, or four—are represented by undotted or dotted notes, according to whether the time is simple or compound. Thus a bar of 2-4 time contains two undotted beats, a bar of 6-8 time two dotted beats, and so on. In compound times, and in simple times when the *tempo* is slow, it is frequently necessary to subdivide each beat into thirds or halves. Slow 6-8 or 9-8 time, for example, may require six or nine beats to the bar, and quick 6-8 or 9-8 time two or three beats. Similarly, slow 2-4 time may require four beats, and quick 2-4 time two beats.

Slow duple-simple time requiring four beats to the bar may be regarded as quadruple time, and beaten as such.[2] (1. Down, 2. Left, 3. Right, 4. Up.) In the compound times the subdivisions are made smaller than the principal beats. In slow 9-8 time, for example, the approximate directions in which the stick moves are as shown in Fig. 16.

---

[1] The click actually serves two purposes: marking the end of one beat and the beginning of the next. Observe that the sound begins at the *bottom* of the down beat.

[2] Thus 2-4 time is regarded as 4-8.

The stick should move farther and more quickly between a principal and a subdivided beat (3 to 4, 6 to 7, and 9 to 1) than between two subdivided beats (1 to 2, 2 to 3, 4 to 5, 5 to 6, etc.), though the actual duration of each beat is the same. If the principal beats are made with the arm or wrist, the subdivided beats should be made with the wrist or fingers.

The directions in which the stick moves when the beat is

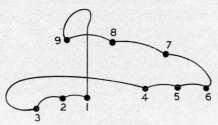

Fig. 16. 9–8 Time

subdivided are as follows (the principal beats are shown in capital letters)—

6 Beats in a Bar

1. DOWN.	2. Left.	3. Left.
4. RIGHT.	5. Right.	6. Up.

8 Beats in a Bar

1. DOWN	2. Right.	3. LEFT.	4. Left
5. RIGHT.	6. Right.	7. UP.	8. Up.

9 Beats in a Bar

1. DOWN.	2. Left.	3. Left.
4. RIGHT.	5. Right.	6. Right.
7. UP.	8. Up.	9. Up.

12 Beats in a Bar

1. DOWN.	2. Right.	3. Right.	4. LEFT.
5. Left.	6. Left.	7. RIGHT.	8. Right.
9. Right.	10. UP.	11. Up.	12. Up.

It is important that one down beat, and one only, shall be given in each bar, so that the performers will be able to distinguish between the first and the other beats of the bar. If, as sometimes happens, the chorus (or principals) make a musical entry too late or too early, unanimity may be restored by giving several quick (or slow) down beats, each representing one bar, until orchestra and chorus have come together again.

Reducing the Beats

In quick duple or triple time it is often necessary to take two or three beats as one, instead of giving each beat separately.

In quick waltz time, for example, it is usual to give only one beat to the bar, except when a *ritenuto* makes a temporary change to three beats desirable.

One in a bar is shown by a single down beat, but (except in the fastest *tempo*) something more than an up and down movement is needed; the stick, after clicking at the bottom of the beat, should rise in a curve, which may be roughly shown as in Fig. 17.

FIG. 17. SINGLE BEAT

In a quick waltz rhythm such as the following, which is five bars of "Valse des Fleurs" (Tchaikovski), any tendency on the part of the orchestra to hurry may be counteracted by marking the first two-thirds of the bar with a down beat, and the last third with an up beat.

In quick quadruple times it is often convenient to take two beats as one, beating two in a bar in the usual way.

When to Subdivide or Reduce the Beats

In deciding whether or not it is desirable to subdivide beats, or to take two or three beats as one, the following points should be taken into consideration—

1. Very quick beats are difficult to follow, and should be avoided as far as possible; on the other hand it is difficult to keep very slow beats steadily moving. In border-line cases, where either slow or quick beats could be given, it is usually better to decide on slow ones.

2. With inexperienced performers it is often advisable to subdivide the beat in the early stages of rehearsal; taking, for example, a quick 2-4 movement in four beats, and changing to two beats when the music is known.

3. It is not always necessary to subdivide every beat of the bar in a slow *tempo*; it is often sufficient to subdivide a particular beat in order to emphasize the rhythm, leaving the other beats undivided.

Five and Seven Beats

Music with five and seven beats to the bar is generally regarded as a combination of duple and triple, or triple and quadruple times, and is beaten according to whether it is grouped as 2 + 3 or 3 + 2 beats, or as 3 + 4 or 4 + 3 beats. The movements of the stick are as follows—

5 BEATS IN A BAR
(2 + 3)

1. DOWN.	2. Left.	3. RIGHT.
4. Right.	5. Up.	

(3 + 2)

1. DOWN.	2. Left.	3. Left.
4. RIGHT.	5. Up.	

7 BEATS IN A BAR
(3 + 4)

1. DOWN.	2. Left.	3. Left.	4. RIGHT.
5. Right.	6. Up.	7. Up.	

(4 + 3)

1. DOWN.	2. Down.	3. Left.	4. Left.
5. RIGHT.	6. Right.	7. Up.	

When beating seven in a bar (4 + 3), the second down beat must be made subordinate to the first (i.e. it must be started from a lower point).

The Preparatory Movement

Before beginning to conduct a piece of music, the conductor must fix in his mind the exact speed at which he is going to beat time. He has then to convey the *tempo* he has chosen to the performers, so that the music shall be started at the correct speed.

Every beat or gesture in conducting requires preparation; the performers cannot be expected to respond to a sudden movement which takes them unawares. If the conductor moves directly from the starting position to the first beat, therefore, they will find it difficult to judge accurately the speed of the first beat. In order to establish the correct *tempo* it is necessary to precede the initial beat with a preparatory movement, which must be made *exactly in the time of one beat*.

If the music begins on the first beat of the bar, the stick should rise in a curve from the starting position, before falling to the down beat.

If the music starts on a beat other than the first of the bar, the preparatory movement should be made in a direction opposite to that of the initial beat.[1] If, when beating four-in-a-bar, for instance, the start is on the second beat, the preparatory movement should be to the right; if the start is on the third beat, the preparatory movement should be to the left, and so on.

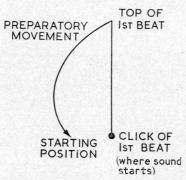

PREPARATORY MOVEMENT

TOP OF 1ST BEAT

STARTING POSITION

CLICK OF 1ST BEAT (where sound starts)

FIG. 18. FIRST BEAT. PREPARATORY

If the music starts on some part of a beat, the preparatory movement may usually be dispensed with, and the actual beat given very distinctly. When the sound starts on or after a beat other than the first, the composer sometimes adds rests to give the initial bar its full value; no preparatory movement is then necessary, the silent beats being given clearly but lightly, and the beat on or after which something is to be played or sung given much more firmly.

Pauses

Before conducting a pause it must be decided exactly how long the note or chord is to be held, and whether it is to be cut off, or followed without a break by the next note or chord. In making these decisions the *tempo* and character of the music must be taken into consideration.

During a pause the stick is held stationary. If the note or chord is to be cut off, the cessation of sound should be indicated by a decisive flick of the stick to the right or left; it is then advisable to make a slight preparatory movement before re-starting (in the direction opposite to that of the beat which follows) to re-establish the *tempo*. If there is to be no cut-off the stick should come to a standstill on the pause, and then move on to the next beat without a break.

[1] The first actual beat given should correspond to the first beat of the music; except in rare instances it is not desirable to give beats or bars "for nothing."

When a pause occurs at the end of a piece, a decisive downward flick of the stick may be used to show when the sound is to be cut off.

The Left Hand

Inexperienced conductors are often at a loss to know what to do with the left hand. They generally find it difficult to overcome the natural tendency of one hand to imitate the other, thus causing movements of the stick to be duplicated by the left hand (the hands, of course, moving in opposite directions for the side beats). When both sides of the theatre orchestra are playing a vigorous passage, it is often desirable to reinforce the rhythm by duplicating the beats, but at other times the left hand should be used only for some definite purpose, such as to indicate *crescendo*, *diminuendo*, *legato*, and *staccato*, and to give entries to voices or instruments. When the left hand is not required it is often convenient to rest it on the music desk, ready to turn over the pages of the score. Although there are no set movements of the left hand, certain gestures are in general use. Thus the outstretched hand, with the palm held upwards or downwards, may be used to indicate a *crescendo* or a *diminuendo*, or to increase or decrease the tone of certain voices or instruments in order to secure a satisfactory balance.

Entries

It is part of a conductor's duty to help his singers and players when they have important entries to make. It is seldom necessary to indicate *every* musical entry. Inexperienced amateurs naturally require more assistance than professionals, who may usually be left to make the less important entries on their own. When several entries occur in quick succession, it is confusing (and sometimes physically impossible) to give each entry separately.

Entries may be given with the stick or with the left hand. Just before giving an entry, the conductor should prepare the performer or performers concerned by looking towards them; the eyes play an important part in conducting, and it is the look as much as the gesture which invites a confident entry. Sometimes, indeed, the look alone is sufficient.

The Conductor's Stand

For reasons of space some orchestra pits have a fixed conductor's desk (often placed at an inconvenient angle) or, where there is a grand Piano in the centre of the orchestra pit, a desk which fits over the top of the Piano. Fixed desks are often unsatisfactory as they cannot be adjusted to suit the height of the conductor. A movable stand is usually the best; it should be fitted with a heavy base so that it is not easily knocked over, and with a solid wooden desk that can be adjusted to any angle.

The conductor should stand sufficiently high for his beat to be seen by the players over the top of their music stands, using, if necessary, a small rostrum or box. He should not stand *too* high, however, or the players immediately beneath him will find difficulty in following his movements. Also, in those theatres or halls which have no centre gangway, he may block the view of the audience in the front centre stalls.

Balance

The theatrical conductor must give his constant attention to the securing of a satisfactory balance between orchestra and voices. It is not always easy to judge the balance from the conductor's desk, and it is sometimes desirable for the leader to take the orchestra through one of the musical numbers at a rehearsal so that the conductor may listen from various parts of the theatre. In securing a good balance the conductor must be guided by the strength of the voice or voices he is accompanying, and must ensure that the words are clearly heard. A very light voice must be lightly accompanied, and it may sometimes be necessary, in certain numbers, to reduce the sound of the orchestra by muting the strings, even if this is not indicated in the score. This may be particularly desirable with amateur players, who usually find considerable difficulty in playing *pianissimo* for any length of time.

The strength of the chorus voices must also be considered. Even when the full company is singing *fortissimo* the balance cannot be taken for granted, as the voices may easily be overpowered by the full weight of the orchestra. If this happens, it is often necessary to mark down the brass parts from, say, *fortissimo* to *mezzo-forte*.

When amateur performances are given in halls where there is no sunk orchestra pit (the players being seated on the same level as the audience), particular attention must be paid to balance, as unless the orchestra plays with restraint the voices may be overpowered.

In addition to the balance between orchestra and voices, the internal balance of the orchestra as a whole must be considered. An orchestra of twelve may contain five string players and three brass; in an orchestra of twenty the strings may be increased to nine, while the brass remain at three. Clearly, then, the smaller number of strings is likely to be overwhelmed by the brass, unless the latter play with considerable discretion; in the larger orchestra, however, the brass will be able to play with a little less restraint. Similar considerations apply to the drums and effects.

Close attention must also be given to all important features of the orchestration. For example, it may be necessary to subdue the strings in order to allow a solo passage for a woodwind instrument to be clearly heard; or, let us say, in a passage in thirds for Flute and Clarinet, to direct the Flute to play a little more loudly than the Clarinet, so that the melody is not obscured by the lower part.

Choice of Tempi

Before starting to conduct a piece of music, the conductor must have in his mind a clear idea of the precise speed at which he is going to start it, and also exactly what alterations of speed —*ritenuto*, *accelerando*—pauses, etc., he intends to make. In deciding the most appropriate speed, he must be guided by the character of the music, and the indications of the composer (*andante*, *allegro*, etc.), and metronome markings ($\quad = 120$, etc.) if any. He must also take into consideration the ability of the singers and instrumentalists under his direction. Very quick music, for example, may have to be taken rather less quickly with amateurs than with professionals. Similarly, very slow music may have to be taken rather less slowly, since amateurs often find difficulty in playing or singing slow, sustained sounds.

The choice of suitable *tempi* is not always an easy one, and it is important that each musical item should be considered as a whole, before a decision is made. If, for example, we have a piece of music which begins with a crotchet rhythm, and subsequently changes to a semiquaver rhythm, it is clear that the speed at which the semiquavers are to be performed must be taken into account; for if the crotchet rhythm only is considered, the *tempo* chosen may prove to be too fast when the semiquaver passage is reached.

The character of the entire musical score must also be considered. A quick-fire musical comedy such as *No, No, Nanette* must proceed at a sparkling pace, and the musical *tempi* must never for a moment be allowed to flag, or the pace of the whole show will be slackened. This means that all cues must be smartly taken up, and that the *tempi* chosen must maintain the general pace of the production, while giving full value to each musical number; it does *not* mean that the music must be raced through at a breakneck speed, in a misguided attempt to achieve a "lively" performance.

Orchestral Accompaniment

An inexperienced conductor will probably adopt too rigid a *tempo* when accompanying singers with the orchestra. In practice as much elasticity as possible should be aimed at, except, of course, when a strictly rhythmic accompaniment is being played. Although a conductor is usually said to "follow" a singer, he must in fact anticipate him; if he tries to follow the notes as they are being sung, the orchestra will invariably be just behind the singer, with the result that the *tempo* of the music will gradually be slowed down. The orchestral accompaniment should therefore be slightly ahead of the singer, but lest this statement should be misinterpreted it must be strongly emphasized that the anticipation must be so slight that neither the singer nor the audience is aware of it. It is really only a question of *thinking* just ahead of the singer, and of accompanying accordingly.

In order to achieve an elastic accompaniment, the conductor should keep his eyes on the singer, giving, where necessary, a fleeting glance to his score, to refresh his memory or to turn a page. Especially should he watch the movements of the lips, for these will tell him exactly when the singer is about to move from one note to the next.

Sometimes, when a singer adopts a *tempo* which is far too slow, it becomes necessary for the conductor to try to lead (or drag) him along. This must be done very gradually, by slightly increasing the speed from bar to bar, until the proper *tempo* is arrived at. It must be sadly confessed, however, that some singers refuse to accept even the most pointed hints from conductor and orchestra, and stick to their self-imposed *tempo* with dogged determination. The most that a conductor can then do is to ensure that orchestra and singer remain in close, even though funereal, company.

Music under Dialogue

Music under dialogue (sometimes called "melos") is often introduced in order to create an atmosphere, and so under-line the sentiment or drama of the action. It must be played very softly, so that the words are not obscured. Muted strings are usually sufficient, or a solo Violin with Piano may be used. Where the volume of sound has suddenly, or gradually, to be increased (when, for example, certain words are shouted, or some dramatic action takes place), extra instruments may have to be added. Sometimes music under dialogue will be played right through; at other times it will be continued until a verbal or visual cue is reached, and then faded out.

Ballet, and Music for Dancing

The precise *tempi* at which music for ballet and other dancing is to be played, must be determined at rehearsal, in consultation with the ballet mistress or dance producer. It is desirable that the musical director should attend as many of the dancing rehearsals as possible, so that he will be able to appreciate the purpose underlying the ballet movements and dance steps. He should also memorize the music, so that during the performance he will be able to give his whole attention to the movements of the dancers.

Finales and Ensembles

Many light operas and musical plays contain long finales, and sometimes other ensembles,[1] in which the full company

---

[1] It is sometimes desirable to cut long finales and ensembles in certain of the older light operas and musical plays, to conform with modern requirements.

takes part. These often include solos, recitative, and concerted
and chorus music, and many sectional rehearsals both of the
principals and the chorus will be necessary before the full
company is brought together. Only by constant and careful
rehearsal will the proper pace of a finale be established, and a
gradual working-up to the climax be achieved. Sometimes a
break will have to be made in a finale, to allow some part of
it to be repeated as an encore; an example of this is found in
the Finale to Act I of *The Gondoliers*, in which part of "A
Regular Royal Queen" is repeated.

The Overture, National Anthem, and Play-out.

Most light operas and musical plays have separate overtures.
In some cases (e.g. *The Arcadians*), the overture is not included
in the vocal score, but will be found in the band parts when
they are hired. Some musical plays (e.g. *The Desert Song*) have
no overture, but only a short prelude which leads straight into
the opening chorus.

The National Anthem may be played either before or after
the performance, according to local custom. If it is given at
the end, it may either be sung by the full company while the
curtain is up, or played by the orchestra after the fall of the
curtain. When an amateur orchestra is employed, it is often
better to provide a printed orchestration.

The National Anthem is usually followed by a "play-out"
or "march-out." Where no special provision for this is made
in the band parts, the orchestra may repeat a refrain of the
final chorus, if this is a bright tune; or a refrain of some other
popular number may be played.

Cues

The conductor should enter, in the vocal score from which
he will conduct, the actual words of the dialogue immediately
preceding each musical number. In addition to the cue for
starting a number, a "warning" cue is sometimes entered; this
consists of some words of dialogue a few lines ahead of the actual
cue, and the purpose is to give the conductor time to alert
his orchestra. It is also desirable that cues should be entered
in the pianist's vocal score. Where cues are visual, the nature
of the stage action or business should be noted in the score.

In addition to marking his cues, the conductor should make himself familiar with the libretto, so that he will be in a position to jump in at once, should the words of a cue be altered or left out. This happens quite often with nervous or inexperienced singers, and sometimes with comedians who are fond of "gagging" (i.e. introducing humour not in the script). Sometimes whole sections of dialogue (and even musical numbers) may be omitted, because of a sudden lapse of memory. Quick thinking, and a knowledge of the libretto and music, are necessary to save such a situation.

When, as sometimes happens, the actual words of a cue are used earlier in the dialogue, the conductor must be careful not to take up the wrong cue. In this example,

A: Come on!
B: What are you going to do?
A: Inform the King. Come on! (MUSIC CUE),

if the conductor starts the music at the first "Come on!" the audience may miss a line of dialogue essential to the plot of the play. This possibility is best avoided by slightly altering the dialogue; when for one reason or another this is not possible, the cue entered in the score should be of sufficient length to distinguish it from the previous dialogue.

When introductory bars are played softly under dialogue, the music and the dialogue must be carefully timed at rehearsal to determine the exact point at which the music should begin. The words of the cue upon which the introduction is to be started should then be entered in the conductor's score. It is often a good plan to write in the remaining dialogue over the introductory music; this will enable the conductor to take the introduction at such a speed that the orchestra will finish it at the precise moment when the performer is ready to sing. In many of the older musical plays, it is often effective to treat the introduction in this way, even though it is not so indicated in the libretto or vocal score.

When the introductory music is played "cold" (i.e. not under dialogue), the conductor should take up his cues smartly, so that no break will occur between the end of the dialogue and the start of the music. It is usually effective to start the introductory music on the last syllable of the spoken dialogue. Occasionally, of course, there must be a deliberate break before the introduction is started, to allow for some movement or stage business.

Some musical numbers have no introductory music, but simply a lead-in note for the singer; this note may be given by a Horn, muted Trumpet, Violin, or Oboe.

It is useful to indicate (in the conductor's score) at the end of each musical number the length of the dialogue which follows (e.g. "Very short dialogue," "10-min. dialogue," etc.). When two numbers follow each other without a break, the word "segue" should be written at the end of the first number, in both the conductor's score and the band parts.

A Sense of the Theatre

A sense of the theatre is to a great extent a natural gift, but much may be learned by experience. It goes without saying that a conductor must, as von Bülow once observed, have "the score in his head, not his head in the score." Occasionally, in cases of illness or other emergency, it is necessary to conduct music at very short notice, or even at sight; the conductor must then do the best he can in difficult circumstances. Normally, however, extensive thought and study should be given to everything he conducts.

If he knows his score well, the conductor will be able to watch everything that is happening on the stage. He will then have to consider exactly how the music is to be played, in order that the dramatic situations may be exploited to the full. Bad timing can easily spoil good music, however well it is played.

A fairly obvious example of the importance of good timing is the fall of the curtain at the end of an Act. Here the music may rise to a triumphant climax, the effect of which may be considerably diminished if the music ceases before the curtain falls, or continues after it has fallen. A similar situation arises when a musical exit is made after the singing of a number; the music must be timed so as to finish at the exact moment that the performer is clear of the stage. Musical entrances need to be timed with equal care.

Stage movements which are intended to coincide with certain bars, or notes of music, are rather more difficult to time. In a show like The Desert Song, for example, much of the action is related to the music, and if the maximum of dramatic effect is to be achieved, complete understanding on the question of timing must exist between the musical director, the producer, and the company.

The successful musical director must be confident, resourceful, and ready for all emergencies. Provision must be made for possible delays in scenic changes; suitable music for such eventualities must be decided on at the orchestral rehearsals, so that the orchestra will know exactly what to play on a pre-arranged signal from the conductor. Such music should on no account consist of the endless repetition of a short piece—a clear indication to the audience that some hitch has occurred.

Quite unexpected changes of *tempi* may sometimes be made by inexperienced singers. In dealing with such contingencies the conductor will find it useful to give quite small beats; they can be more easily adapted to sudden changes of *tempi* than large ones.

Finally, the conductor should get to know the musical habits and failings of musicians in general, and of the singers and players under his direction in particular; he will then be in a position to anticipate their shortcomings, and thus avert many catastrophes before they come upon him.

THE ORCHESTRAL REHEARSALS

The musical director of an amateur production is likely to have under his control an orchestra of amateurs alone, or of amateurs with a stiffening of professionals; or, if he is lucky, an existing professional orchestra of the type usually found in provincial theatres. In the latter case, the orchestral rehearsals may, for reasons of expense, have to be limited to the three-hour band call which is usual in professional touring productions. Whenever possible, however, two orchestral rehearsals should be regarded as the absolute minimum for an amateur production, even if a professional orchestra is employed. An orchestra of amateur players will usually require considerably more rehearsal.

If only two rehearsals are possible, the first should be for the orchestra alone, and the second should be a music rehearsal for the entire company with orchestra. The dress rehearsal is often accompanied only by the Piano. The presence of an orchestra is, of course, a great advantage, but a dress rehearsal often lasts six hours or more, and it is usually not possible for the orchestra to remain throughout this period. Moreover, a dress rehearsal should not be regarded as a rehearsal for the orchestra; the producer must concentrate on the production as a whole, and the orchestra would inevitably have to remain idle during a large part of the proceedings.

If there are to be two or more rehearsals for the orchestra alone, the first will usually be devoted to playing the music right through, for the purpose of eliminating wrong notes and inaccuracies of time. At the remaining rehearsals, details of ensemble, expression, style, and interpretation will claim attention. To a great extent, however, the procedure will depend on the ability of the players, With amateurs in general, a good deal of attention will have to be paid to the correction of faulty execution, and only when the music is familiar will it be possible to tackle the finer points of style and interpretation. Professional players, on the other hand, will usually be able to play their parts without much difficulty, and their wider experience will enable them to respond more quickly than amateurs to the suggestions of the conductor.

Well in advance of the first rehearsal, the conductor should examine the band parts to ensure that they are in order, to eliminate any conflicting directions which may have been marked in by previous users, and to make a mental note of any passages which are likely to prove specially difficult for the players. He should also see that, if possible, rehearsal letters (or numbers) are provided at convenient points; these save valuable time, for when the orchestra has to be stopped, the place where a restart is to be made can be quickly indicated by saying "Six bars before letter B," and so on.

Since the period of orchestral rehearsals is likely to be limited, and much has to be done, the conductor must know how to make the best possible use of the time at his disposal. Rehearsals should start punctually at the time appointed, and the short break for the musicians should not be allowed to become a long one. Before each number is rehearsed for the first time, the conductor should clarify, as briefly as possible, any points on which there may be misunderstanding, such as (a) the number of verses and refrains to be played; (b) which

repeats, if any, are to be observed, and which are to be ignored;
(c) where the encore, if any, is to be started; and (d) how many
beats to the bar will be given,[1] in cases where reasonable doubt
might exist.

When rehearsing, the conductor should stop the orchestra
only when absolutely necessary. Players quickly lose patience
if they are pulled up every few bars or so, and also much time
is wasted. Obvious mistakes (such as the omission of accidentals) can usually be corrected without stopping the
orchestra, by a word to the players concerned; points of
balance, expression, and style can often be indicated in the
same way, by words such as "attack," "smoothly," "softer,"
"full bows," "less brass," "let the Flute through," and so on.

Amateur string players usually need to be encouraged to
make confident entries in loud passages, and to be restrained
from playing too loudly in softer ones; amateur brass players
and drummers will often be found to have similar failings.

In conducting an existing professional theatre orchestra, the
inexperienced conductor will find that the musicians, if
approached with consideration and tact, will usually be glad
to give him all the help and advice he needs. Any suggestion
of truculence or superiority will, however, be strongly resented,
and the lack of co-operation resulting from such an attitude
may well prevent the conductor from securing the results he
desires.

It should be noted that fast music can usually be taken at a
slightly slower *tempo* at rehearsals than at a performance; the
excitement and nervous tension which will inevitably be felt
when an audience is present will allow the music to be carried
along a little faster than at, say, the dress rehearsal, where a
general feeling of flatness usually predominates.

---

[1] During actual rehearsal or performance, it is sometimes useful to indicate
the number of beats with the fingers of the left hand; this is often desirable when
deputy players are present, who may be unfamiliar with the score.

CHAPTER NINE

THE THEATRE ORCHESTRA

THERE is no standard combination for the theatre orchestra; the size and the choice of instruments must depend on (*a*) the orchestral requirements of the light opera, musical comedy, etc., in question, (*b*) the number of musicians available, and (*c*) financial considerations.

THE COMBINATION OF THE THEATRE ORCHESTRA

Ideally, the orchestra for any musical production should contain all the instruments specified in the original score. The combination of instruments varies according to the nature of the work, but it may be useful to give some examples, which are typical of many of the musical productions frequently given by amateur societies.

The Arcadians (Lionel Monckton and Howard Talbot)

The original scoring is for Strings (1st Violins, 2nd Violins, Violas, 'Cellos, and Basses), Flute, Oboe, two Clarinets, Bassoon, two Horns, two Cornets (Trumpets), Trombone, and Drums.

Miss Hook of Holland (Paul Rubens)

As for *The Arcadians*, but with two Flutes.

The Mikado and *Iolanthe* (Arthur Sullivan)

As for *The Arcadians*, but with two Flutes and two Tenor Trombones.

The Gondoliers and *The Yeomen of the Guard* (Arthur Sullivan)

As for *The Arcadians*, but with two Flutes, two Bassoons, and three Trombones (two Tenor and one Bass).

The Student Prince (Sigmund Romberg)

As for *The Arcadians*, but with two Flutes, two Trombones, and Harp. (*N.B.* The Bassoon part is optional.)

Merrie England (Edward German)

As for *The Arcadians*, but with two Flutes, three Trombones, and Harp.

The Three Musketeers (Rudolf Friml)

As for *The Arcadians*, but with two Flutes, two Bassoons, three Trumpets, two Trombones, and Harp.

Viktoria and Her Hussar (Paul Abrahams)

Strings, Tenor Banjo, Flute (doubling B-Flat Tenor Saxophone), two Clarinets (doubling E-Flat Alto Saxophones), Bassoon, two Trumpets, two Trombones, Drums, Harp, and Orchestral Piano.

Bless the Bride (Vivian Ellis)

Strings, Flute, Oboe, two Clarinets, two Trumpets, two Trombones, Drums, Harp, and Orchestral Piano.

It should be noted that in all but two of the above orchestrations the Piano is not included. Ideally, the number of string players would be about six 1st Violins, four 2nd Violins, three Violas, two 'Cellos, and one or two Basses. The complete orchestra for *Miss Hook of Holland* would therefore number twenty-eight or twenty-nine players. Very few amateur operatic societies are fortunate enough to be able to employ such an orchestra. The smaller orchestra which they must use will therefore of necessity be incomplete, and a pianist must be introduced to fill in, as far as possible, the parts of those instruments which are missing.

Some of the bigger societies are able to take over a local theatre for their productions, together with the existing orchestra of professional musicians. The combination of such an orchestra varies with the size of the theatre, but where there is a resident orchestra it is usual to find from ten to twelve musicians who are accustomed to playing together as a team, and are therefore able to give a reasonably efficient interpretation of the music which is put before them. The average professional theatre of twelve musicians is made up of: Piano, three Violins, 'Cello, Bass, Flute, Clarinet, two Trumpets, Tenor Trombone, and Drums. If funds permit, the larger societies may be in a position to augment such an orchestra for their productions, and the professional resident musical director or manager at the theatre will usually be able to secure additional players if they are available.

When a society is not able to take over a professional orchestra, a special orchestra must be collected and rehearsed for the production. This will consist either of local professionals (or semi-professionals), or of amateurs, or of amateurs strengthened by a few professionals. If amateurs are included, it is important that only players of known ability should be chosen. Quality must not be sacrificed to quantity—six really capable musicians are infinitely to be preferred to sixteen indifferent players. If good amateur woodwind, horn, and brass players cannot be found, and there are no professionals available, it is better to dispense with the wind section entirely than to employ bad players. In a small orchestra, consisting of strings and Piano only, a Mustel Organ or a Harmonium (played by a capable musician) is often useful for filling in missing parts for woodwind and horns.

FROM ONE TO THIRTY PLAYERS

The list which follows gives the *suggested* combination of an orchestra of from one to thirty players. An orchestra (if it may be so called) of one will therefore consist of a Piano; an orchestra of two of a Piano and a Violin; an orchestra of three of a Piano, a Violin, and a 'Cello; and so on. In adding one instrument to an orchestra of nineteen, it is suggested that the Piano be dropped and two Horns added, making twenty players in all. In a large orchestra, the thirtieth instrument could be either a Harp, a second Oboe, or a second Bassoon, according to the requirements of the score.

1.	Piano.	10.	Trumpet.
2.	Violin.	11.	Tenor Trombone.
3.	'Cello.	12.	2nd Trumpet.
4.	Bass.	13.	Violin.
5.	Violin.	14.	Oboe.
6.	Clarinet.	15.	Viola.
7.	Flute (Piccolo).	16.	Violin.
8.	Drums (including Timpani).	17.	2nd Clarinet.
		18.	Violin.
9.	Violin.	19.	Bassoon.

20. 1st and 2nd Horns (omit-
      ting Piano).
21. Violin.
22. 2nd Tenor Trombone.
23. Viola.
24. Violin.
25. 'Cello.

26. 2nd Flute.
27. Violin.
28. 2nd Bass.
29. Bass Trombone.
30. Harp (or 2nd Oboe, or
      2nd Bassoon).

The suggested combinations should suit the average musical play, Gilbert and Sullivan opera, etc., but it must be remembered that some orchestrations do not include a second Flute part, and may be scored not for three Trombones, but for one or two; also that certain orchestrations feature the Piano as a solo instrument[1] (it cannot therefore be omitted under any circumstances), and also instruments only occasionally used in the theatre orchestra, such as the Cor Anglais, the Bass Clarinet, and the Tuba. Also, in dance shows the brass section may contain three Trumpets,[2] and the Horns may be discarded in favour of Saxophones.

It should be noted that no more than four brass are normally used in an orchestra of twenty-eight players; the Bass Trombone should be added only when the strings and woodwind are at full strength.

In small song and dance shows, revues, etc., the usual orchestra is sometimes replaced by a trio consisting of two Pianos and Drums. With two competent pianists capable of playing together, and a resourceful and discreet drummer, this combination will often prove surprisingly successful.

THE STRING SECTION

The string section consists of 1st Violins, 2nd Violins, Violas, 'Cellos, and Double-Basses. Basically the strings are written in four parts, the 1st Violins playing the top part, the 2nd Violins and Violas the two inner parts, and the 'Cellos and Basses the lowest part in octaves. Often, however, the 'Cellos play an independent melodic part, thus making five parts in all, and sometimes any or all of the parts which make up the string

[1] The Piano is essential in *Viktoria and Her Hussar* (Paul Abrahams), and in *Bless the Bride* (Vivian Ellis).
   Some of the early dance shows included two pianos in the orchestration, and in the original production of *Lady Luck* (Richard Rodgers) four Pianos were used.
[2] Three Trumpets are also used in some of the larger romantic musical shows, e.g. *The Three Musketeers* (Rudolf Friml) and *The Vagabond King* (Rudolf Friml).

section are divided. (The 1st Violins, in particular, often play in two or more parts.)

The four strings of the Violin, Viola, 'Cello, and Bass are tuned thus—

The notes shown above are those produced by the "open" strings, i.e. by strings which are not stopped by the fingers. "Stopping" is effected by pressing a string down on the finger-board with a finger; the string is thus shortened and a higher note obtained. By stopping with the first four fingers of the left hand, a complete chromatic scale may be produced. Further-more, by moving the hand up the neck of the instrument, in stages called "positions," the upward compass may be ex-tended, and many alternative methods of fingering obtained. (Amateur string players of limited technique are often dis-concerted when asked to play in the highest positions, and it is sometimes as well to let them play very high passages an octave lower than written, provided, of course, that the harmony is not thereby impaired.)

The upward compass of the string section is determined by the ability of the players, so that there is no precise upward limit. The following may be taken as the approximate compass of each instrument (the lowest note being that produced by the lowest open string of the instrument concerned)—

Violin: $3\frac{1}{2}$ octaves   Viola: $3\frac{1}{4}$ octaves
'Cello: $3\frac{1}{4}$ octaves   Bass: $2\frac{1}{2}$ octaves

In a complete theatre orchestra of thirty musicians, the fifteen or sixteen string players would probably be organized as follows—

6 1st Violins   3 (or 4) 2nd Violins
2 Violas   2 'Cellos   2 Basses

In smaller orchestras the number of string players would be considerably reduced, an orchestra of from ten to twelve players probably containing three 1st Violins, one 'Cello and one Bass, but no Violas. With such a combination it is desirable to have three 1st Violins (rather than two 1st Violins and one 2nd Violin), as two players in unison will not produce good orchestral tone, and may tend to sound out of tune. The inner parts (2nd Violin and Viola) will therefore have to be filled in by the Piano.

The conductor who has had no practical experience of string playing should make himself familiar with the various points of string technique which follow.

Chords

Two notes on adjacent strings may be sounded at the same time, producing two-part chords, and known as "double-stopping." Three-part and four-part chords may also be played almost simultaneously (each note being on a different string), although only the upper two notes can be sustained. On the Violin and the Viola numerous double-stops are possible, though some are more difficult to play than others. The easiest double-stops are those in which an open string is combined with a stopped or open note on a string immediately above or below it; where both notes are stopped the larger intervals—fifths, sixths, sevenths, and octaves—are easier than the smaller ones. On the 'Cello fewer double-stops are available, perfect fifths and major and minor sixths being the easiest. The Bass is seldom called upon to play chords of any kind.

Notation

Music for the Violin is written entirely in the treble clef; music for the Viola is written in the alto clef, with the occasional use of the treble clef for the higher passages. Three clefs are used for 'Cello music: the bass clef for the lower notes, and the tenor and treble clefs for the higher ones. Music for the Bass is normally written in the bass clef, though the tenor clef is sometimes used for very high passages. It is important to note that whereas the Violin, Viola, and 'Cello are non-transposing instruments (i.e. the written notes sound at their actual pitch), music for the Bass always sounds an octave lower than the written notes.

Bowing

When two or more notes are intended to be played in the same bow, they are covered by a slur. Notes not covered by a slur are played with alternate "down" and "up" bows. A down bow (from heel to point) may be indicated by the sign ⊓, and an up bow (from point to heel) by the sign ∨.

Notes covered by a slur are played absolutely *legato* (i.e. without any break); when, however, slurred notes have (*a*) dots 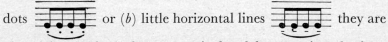 or (*b*) little horizontal lines they are played in one bow, but are articulated by stopping the bow between each note, the notes being (*a*) short (*staccato*), and (*b*) long. Notes not covered by a slur are played *legato* with separate bows. Unslurred notes with dots over them are played *staccato*; at quick speed they may also be played *spiccato*, a very light stroke made with a bouncing bow. Very firm, detached notes are played *martellato*, with a quick pushing or pulling stroke at the point of the bow.

The many varieties of bowing cannot be adequately conveyed by mere description, and the conductor with no knowledge of the subject would do well to ask some friendly and experienced string player to demonstrate them. Really first-class string playing can be achieved only when all the players in the same string group use similar bowing; the Leader (i.e. the principal 1st Violin), if he is competent, will be able to advise the conductor on all matters of bowing affecting the Violins, and to ensure that they all follow the bowing decided on.

Other Points of String Technique

Tremolo. The rapid reiteration of the same note (or double-stop) is called *bow-tremolo*, written thus 〔♪〕. The rapid alteration of two notes on the same string is called *finger-tremolo*, written thus: 〔♪〕.

Pizzicato (or *pizz*). This Italian word indicates that the string is to be plucked with the finger, instead of being played with the bow. The word *arco* indicates that bowing is to be resumed.

Con sordini (or *Con sord.*) indicates that a mute is to be placed on the bridge, to deaden the quality of the tone; *Senza sordini* indicates its removal. The English "mutes" and "mutes off" is also used.

Col legno, rarely used in the theatre, indicates that the strings are to be struck with the back of the bow, producing a dry rattle.

Sul ponticello produces a special tone-colour—hard and glassy —obtained by playing with the bow near the bridge.

Sul tasto produces a very light feathery tone, the bow being drawn on or near the finger-board.

THE WOODWIND SECTION

The woodwind section in the full theatre orchestra consists of one or two Flutes (one player doubling Piccolo when required), one (or occasionally two) Oboes (one player sometimes doubling Cor Anglais where this is represented in the score), two Clarinets (one sometimes doubling Bass Clarinet), and one or two Bassoons. In smaller combinations of from ten to fourteen players, only one Flute, one Clarinet, and possibly one Oboe will be employed. In recruiting amateur woodwind players, care must be taken to ensure that they possess modern low-pitch instruments; some of the old high-pitched instruments still exist, and cannot be tuned down satisfactorily. While many quite competent amateur Flute and Clarinet players are to be found, good Oboe and Bassoon players are decidedly scarce. Inefficient players should be avoided at all costs, as more often than not they will be found to be more trouble than they are worth.

The *written* compass of the woodwind group is as follows—

Flute and Piccolo

The Flute is a non-transposing instrument,[1] the music being written in the treble clef. It is remarkably agile, and most

[1] i.e. the music sounds as it is written.

trills, rapid scale passages, arpeggios, and double and triple tonguing are easy and effective.

The Piccolo is pitched an octave above the Flute, the music being written an octave below the real sounds. The tone is shrill and penetrating. Provided that it is not heard too frequently, the Piccolo may often be used with excellent effect in bright chorus numbers. When a single player is employed, he will change from Flute to Piccolo, as required.

Oboe and Cor Anglais

The Oboe, also non-transposing, is a double-reed instrument, and is therefore less agile than the Flute. The penetrating, somewhat nasal, tone makes it the ideal melodic instrument.

The Cor Anglais[1] (or English Horn) is neither English nor a Horn, being a large Oboe pitched a fifth below the normal instrument. The part is written in the treble clef, a perfect fifth above the real sounds, and therefore sounds a perfect fifth lower than written.

Clarinet

The Clarinet is a single-reed transposing instrument. Each player has two instruments, one in B flat and one in A, for each of which the *written* compass is that already shown. The treble clef is used, and the notes sound a tone lower than written for the B-flat Clarinet, and a minor third lower than written for the A Clarinet. The key-signatures are altered accordingly; in the key of C Major, for example, the B-flat Clarinet would have a signature of two sharps (D Major), and the A Clarinet a signature of three flats (E flat Major). The choice of one or other of the two instruments is made with a view to avoiding a large number of sharps or flats in the key-signature; in the key of E Major, for instance, the composer would choose the A Clarinet, with a signature of one sharp (G Major), rather than the B-flat Clarinet, with a signature of six sharps (F sharp Major)—and so on.

Many players in theatre orchestras invariably use the B-flat Clarinet throughout, making the necessary transposition where music for the A Clarinet is encountered. Amateur players, some of whom possess only a B-flat instrument, often find

[1] Oboe (doubling Cor Anglais) is used in *Bless the Bride* (Vivian Ellis).

difficulty in making such a transposition, and it then becomes necessary to have any music for the A Clarinet transposed to suit the B-flat instrument.

The Clarinet is very agile, and quick passages based on arpeggio figures are frequently written, and easily executed. Rapid chromatic passages, however, are less suited to the character of the instrument.

The Bass Clarinet makes a rare appearance in the theatre orchestra, when it is usually played by the second Clarinet player. It is pitched in B-flat, an octave below the usual B-flat instrument. The part is written either in the treble clef a major ninth above the actual sounds, or in the bass clef a tone above the actual sounds.

Bassoon

The Bassoon is a double-reed instrument, and is non-transposing. Its normal function is to provide the bass of the woodwind group, but it is also used for solo passages, its dry staccato being frequently exploited by composers to produce humorous effects. The part is written in the bass clef, or (for high passages) in the tenor clef.

Horns

Horns are usually to be found only in the full theatre orchestra—they generally play in pairs, though it is possible to obtain excellent effects from a single horn. Before the invention of valves, Horns were provided with a series of detachable "crooks" in all keys. Nowadays the valve-horn is always pitched in the key of F, the written compass being—

Music for the Horn in F is written in the treble or bass clef, a perfect fifth higher than the actual pitch, so that the compass in real sounds is a perfect fifth lower than that given above. In older scores (including the Gilbert and Sullivan operas) the composer sometimes wrote for Horns in keys other than F; in such cases the following table of transpositions will be found useful.

Horn in B flat (alto) is written a major 2nd above the real sounds.
Horn in A is written a minor 3rd above the real sounds.
Horn in A flat is written a major 3rd above the real sounds.
Horn in G is written a perfect 4th above the real sounds.
Horn in E is written a minor 6th above the real sounds.
Horn in E flat is written a major 6th above the real sounds.
Horn in D is written a minor 7th above the real sounds.
Horn in C is written an octave above the real sounds.
Horn in B flat (basso) is written a major 9th above the real sounds.

Horn parts are often written without a key-signature, accidentals being inserted when required; some modern composers use the correct key-signatures, however, and nowadays there is no good reason for not doing so. On the old valveless Horn, chromatic notes were produced by inserting the right hand in the bell of the instrument; this device, known as "stopping," is still used on occasions when a different quality of sound is wanted. A small cross (+) placed over a note indicates that it is to be stopped; where several notes are involved the word "stopped" is used, followed by *naturel* when normal playing is to be resumed. A somewhat similar sound can be produced by placing a mute in the bell of the instrument (indicated by the word "mute" or *con sordini*).

Saxophones

Parts for one or more Saxophones are to be found in the scores of many dance shows. As the tone of the Saxophone tends to obscure the lyrics when used as an accompaniment to a solo voice, Saxophone players are often required to play on Clarinets, or other woodwind instruments, for solo numbers, changing to Saxophones for chorus numbers and dance routines.

Saxophones are made in several different sizes, but the *written* compass is the same for each instrument—

The E-flat Alto Saxophone sounds a major sixth lower than written.

The B-flat Tenor Saxophone sounds a major ninth (i.e. an octave and a tone) lower than written.

The E-flat Baritone Saxophone sounds a major thirteenth lower than written (i.e. an octave lower than the E-flat Alto).

The number and types of Saxophones used vary in different scores. When there is only one Saxophone, the E-flat Alto is usually chosen; when there are two, the E-flat Alto and the B-flat Tenor; and when there are three, two E-flat Altos and one B-flat Tenor. With four Saxophones, there are sometimes two E-flat Altos and two B-flat Tenors, and sometimes two E-flat Altos, one B-flat Tenor, and one E-flat Baritone.

In the dance style of orchestration the different groups of instruments—Saxophones, brass, and strings—are frequently written in close harmony, the group (or a combination of different groups) being supported by a rhythmic accompaniment (Piano, Guitar, Bass, Drums, etc.).

Where good Alto or Tenor Saxophone players are available, but Saxophone parts are not included in the score, Horn parts may often be played by the Saxophones with good effect, if the necessary transpositions are made. Music for Horns in F would need to be written a tone higher for the E-flat Alto Saxophone, and a perfect fifth higher for the B-flat Tenor Saxophone.

THE BRASS SECTION

The brass section of the theatre orchestra usually consists of one of the following combinations:

(a) 2 Trumpets and 1 Tenor Trombone.
(b) 2 Trumpets and 2 Tenor Trombones.
(c) 2 Trumpets, 2 Tenor Trombones, and 1 Bass Trombone.

In smaller orchestras there may be only one Trumpet and one Tenor Trombone (in which case the brass harmony will sound rather thin), while in several well-known dance-shows three Trumpets, and one, two, or three Trombones are called for.

In addition to playing their own parts, the brass section can often be usefully employed (during periods when they would otherwise be resting) in playing the parts of Horns and other wind instruments which may be missing from an incomplete orchestra. To facilitate this, brass parts are sometimes provided with small "cue" notes, to be played when the instrument named is not represented. When brass parts are not so cued, it is often worth while to write in important wind passages, in the absence of which the orchestration would sound thin or incomplete. Short passages of cue notes can often be inserted by clipping a strip of music paper to the part (with paper clips). Woodwind and Horn cues must be played with discretion, however, and an unobtrusive effect is often more easily obtained if the brass players use their mutes.

Trumpets (and Cornets)

In the modern theatre the B-flat Trumpet is normally used, though sometimes, in extreme sharp keys, it is put into A, by means either of a valve or of a detachable short shank.

The *written* compass in either case is .

The actual sounds of the B-flat Trumpet are a tone lower than written, and of the A Trumpet a minor third lower (as in the case of the Clarinets). In many of the older scores, including the Gilbert and Sullivan operas, Cornets are used in place of Trumpets, though nowadays the Cornet parts are often played on Trumpets. Both instruments have precisely the same compass, and by means of single, double, and triple tonguing can perform extremely rapid passages; certain shakes, which are made with the valves, are also possible and effective. The tone of the Cornet, however, is more mellow, and less brassy, than that of the Trumpet.

Mutes can be applied to both instruments. The normal (or straight) mute produces a beautiful, distant effect when the instrument is blown softly, and a fierce, grotesque sound when it is blown loudly. Other kinds of Trumpet mutes are sometimes used for special effects; the "hush" mute gives a very soft unobtrusive sound, while the "wa-wa" mute is provided with a small orifice, which may be opened and closed by the hand to produce two kinds of tone.

Trombones

The Tenor Trombone in B flat, and the Bass Trombone in G are both non-transposing instruments, the actual sounds being the same as the written notes.

The compass is—

Tenor Trombone    Bass Trombone

The slide can be placed in seven positions, each of which produces a different series of sounds (known as harmonics). In the first position (with the slide unextended) on the Tenor Trombone, the following notes can be obtained:

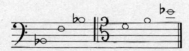

In the second position a series of notes a semitone below the above is obtainable, and so on until the seventh position is reached (with the slide fully extended), when the series of notes will be a diminished fifth below those obtainable in the first position. If the series of notes obtainable in all seven positions is written out, it will be seen that certain notes can be obtained in more than one position; it will also be appreciated that certain sequences of notes are almost impossible to play at high speed (e.g. the lowest note of the Tenor Trombone, followed by the B flat immediately above it, involves a change of slide from the seventh to the first position).

Short glissandos, sometimes used for humorous effects, can be produced by rapid movements of the slide; the utmost limit for these is a diminished fifth (i.e. from the first position to the seventh, or vice versa).

In the theatre, music for the Trombones is usually written in the bass clef throughout, though the tenor clef is sometimes used for the Tenor Trombone. The Trombones can be muted in the same way as the Trumpets.

Tuba

The orchestral Tuba in F is rarely found in the theatre orchestra.[1] It is non-transposing, with the compass—

The usual function of the Tuba is to reinforce the bass of the brass group, or to bring some important bass passage into prominence.

DRUMS AND EFFECTS

The percussion section of the theatre orchestra is usually represented by a single player, playing from a composite part which shows the whole of the percussion effects required. The instruments used will vary with the requirements of the score, and the equipment of the player. The average drummer will be provided with a pair of Timpani (Kettledrums), Side Drum, Bass Drum, Cymbals, and sundry smaller instruments and effects such as the Triangle, the Tambourine, and the Wood Block. He may or may not possess a Xylophone, a Glockenspiel, and a Vibraphone (useful instruments for lending colour to a score); and where less usual instruments are vital to the production (e.g. the Chimes in *Les Cloches de Corneville*) these may have to be specially hired. In very small orchestra pits there may be insufficient space to accommodate all the percussion instruments, and one or both Timpani may have to be sacrificed. This is unfortunate, for in most musical shows the Timpani part is important, and gives useful body to a small orchestra. When Timpani are not available, or cannot be accommodated, the Timpani part may often be played with quite good effect on the Bass Drum, Timpani sticks being used for the purpose. In the purely dance type of show, however, the Timpani often fulfil a less important function.

Amateur drummers (as well as some professionals) may have to be restrained from playing too loudly; a nervous drummer,

---

[1] Effective use is made of the Tuba, however, throughout the score of *Carousel* (Richard Rodgers).

on the other hand, may need encouragement to play a little more boldly. Any tendency to "force the pace" when playing quick movements on the Side Drum, etc., must be firmly checked.

In comedy numbers and dance routines, a resourceful drummer (who should have a clear view of the stage) can usually be relied on to provide effects that will give point to the score, but here again over-enthusiasm may have to be curbed. Where special effects are wanted, it is always wise to arrange these with the drummer at the orchestral rehearsals, and to indicate them in the drum part (e.g. WOOD BLOCK when comedian, knitting, drops stitches, BASS DRUM for fall, etc.). And until the drummer is familiar with the show, the conductor should look towards him a moment or two before each effect is required, in order to give him his cue; this is usually best given with the left hand.

Timpani

Two drums are normally used in the theatre orchestra. The smaller drum can be tuned to any note between ♮ and the larger drum between ♮. A third drum, used in symphony orchestras but rarely found in the theatre, can be tuned from G to D, or if smaller from A to E. The notes to which the Timpani are to be tuned are indicated at the beginning of a movement (e.g. TIMP. in G,D.). During the course of a movement the tuning may be altered (e.g. Change TIMP. to A,E.); such a change takes some little time to effect, during which the drummer is, of course, fully occupied, and cannot play. The Timpani are struck with a pair of flexible, felt-headed sticks. The part is written in the bass clef, without a key-signature. The roll is indicated either by *tr. . . .* over a note, or by ♩.

Side Drum, Bass Drum, Cymbals, and Wood Block

These instruments, all of indefinite pitch, are usually played by a single drummer. The Side Drum is normally played with hardwood sticks; the tightness of the drumhead enables a very close roll to be obtained by a series of doubletaps with each stick. Lighter Side Drum rhythms can also be played with wire brushes, an effect often used in dance shows.

The Bass Drum is played by means of a foot pedal to which a cymbal striker is fitted; this striker can be adjusted to allow either the Bass Drum and Cymbal to be played together, or the Bass Drum to be played alone. In addition, a loose Cymbal is suspended above the Bass Drum; this may be struck with a Side Drum stick (the Cymbal being usually "damped" with the hand immediately it is struck); or with the Timpani stick (an effective roll may be performed with two Timpani sticks); or with wire brushes.

The Wood Block is played with Side Drum sticks; there are also "Temple Blocks" of different sizes, which can be used to produce "horses' hooves," and similar effects.

The Bass Drum part is usually written in the lowest space of the bass stave, and the pedal Cymbal in the space next above; the Side Drum is then placed in the fourth space, and the Wood Block, etc., in the top space. The use of the loose Cymbal is usually indicated by a diamond-shaped note $\left(\, \diamond \,\right)$ placed anywhere on the stave; a roll is shown by *tr. . . .* above a note.

Triangle, Tambourine, and Castanets

The Triangle is a metal bar bent into a triangular shape. It must be struck with a metal beater (the use of the Side Drum stick should not be tolerated). A roll can be produced by striking rapidly between two sides of the Triangle.

The Tambourine may be played in several ways; it may be struck sharply with the fist, or lightly with the fingers; or it may be shaken, when only the jingles will be heard; or the vellum may be rubbed with the thumb, causing the jingles to vibrate.

Orchestral Castanets are usually mounted on an ebony handle, for ease of playing.

Music for the Triangle, Tambourine, and Castanets is usually written on the treble stave, in any convenient space.

Other effects occasionally used include Sleigh Bells, Chimes (or Tubular Bells) usually consisting of eight or thirteen tubes giving the major or chromatic scale of E flat, Gongs, and Tom-Toms.

Glockenspiel, Xylophone, and Vibraphone

The Glockenspiel consists of a series of little metal bars which, when struck with small hammers, produce a fairy-like tinkle. Some Glockenspiels are fitted with a keyboard action, and resemble a small Piano. The written compass is usually about two octaves upwards from middle C, the notes sounding two octaves higher than written.

The Xylophone[1] consists of a series of wooden bars which are struck with small beaters. The tone is dry and hard, and rapid passages, glissandos, etc., can be played with great rapidity. The compass (sounding as written) is usually two octaves and a tone, upwards from B flat on the third line of the treble stave.

The Vibraphone is a Xylophone fitted with metal bars, under which resonators are fitted. Each resonator has a small fan, the series of fans being set in motion by an electric motor. Single notes, and chords of two, three, and four notes can be played; the tone is mellow and sustained. The compass (sounding as written) is usually about two octaves, upwards from middle C.

THE HARP

The Harp has a place in the score of many of the "romantic" musical plays, such as *Betty in Mayfair*, *The Desert Song*, *Music in the Air*, and *Bitter Sweet*. It is not used in shows such as *Miss Hook of Holland*, *The Arcadians*, or the Gilbert and Sullivan operas. Good harpists are rare, and as the Harp is in any case a "luxury" instrument (the part can be more or less satisfactorily supplied by a good pianist) it is not often found in the orchestras of amateur societies. It will suffice to mention, therefore, that Harp music is written on two staves like Piano music; that chords, arpeggios, and glissandos are frequently used; and that the Harp which is tuned to the diatonic scale of C flat is provided with seven pedals, by means of which each note of the scale can be raised either a semitone or a tone—it is therefore non-chromatic by nature.

[1] There is an important part for Xylophone in *The Vagabond King* (Rudolf Friml).

THE ORCHESTRAL PIANIST

Good rehearsal pianists are also rare, and good orchestral pianists rarer. Yet the pianist is (or ought to be) the backbone of the small theatre orchestra. His chief function is to supply a good middle (which would otherwise be lacking in an orchestra without 2nd Violins and Violas), and to reinforce the bass. This means that instead of playing the Piano part exactly as it is printed in the vocal score, he should be able to provide a suitable accompaniment at sight, using the printed part simply as a guide to the harmony. This Piano part, eight bars of "Love Comes from the Heart" (by kind permission of Goodwin and Tabb, Ltd.), for example,

might be played thus—

The tone of the Piano does not blend well with that of the other instruments of the orchestra, and the pianist should try to make his accompaniment as unobtrusive as possible. Melody parts (played, say, by the Violins or a Flute) should normally be left out, but the pianist must keep a watchful eye on the score as a whole, and be ready to play anything of importance that may inadvertently be missed out. Some knowledge of harmony and orchestration is therefore very desirable.

Some orchestrations include a "piano-conductor" part, consisting of an accompaniment on two staves (which can be played as it is written), with the melody cued in small notes either on a third stave or on the right-hand stave.

In a larger orchestra, where the instrumentation is more or

less complete, the pianist can concentrate on filling in the parts of missing instruments, such as the Harp.

THE ORCHESTRA PIT

The arrangement of the players in an orchestra pit will vary according to the size and shape of the pit, and the height of the stage. Where the pit is large, wide, and deep, few difficulties should arise. Many pits are too small, however, to accommodate the number of players desired, and it is then necessary either to reduce the size of the orchestra or to enlarge the pit by removing one or more rows of stalls. Sometimes, in small pits, the brass players and the drummer sit in the stage boxes on either side of the pit, but this arrangement is seldom very satisfactory. Occasionally the drummer (and the harpist, if one is employed) may be accommodated outside the pit, but this is often not possible because of local regulations governing the obstruction of gangways, etc. The main considerations in arranging an orchestra pit are that all the players shall be comfortably seated (string players must have adequate space for bowing, and Trombones sufficient room to extend their slides), and that they shall all have a clear view of the conductor.

In halls where the orchestra pit has be to improvised, and is therefore not sunk, care must be taken to provide music stands and lights which do not project above the stage, and so obscure the view of the audience. Where large stands with fixed shaded lights are used, it may be necessary for the conductor to stand on a small rostrum, in order that his movements can be clearly seen by the players over the tops of their stands.

Where a Piano is used, it is generally placed in the centre of the pit. Though this arrangement may make it difficult for the conductor to judge the balance of the orchestra as a whole, it has the advantage of bringing the pianist and the conductor in close contact with one another, so that conversation is possible in case of emergency. In an orchestra of experienced players, however, the Piano can be placed at the extreme end of the pit, if this is more convenient. When an upright Piano is used in an improvised pit, this may, in fact, be essential, as if placed in the middle the Piano may project above the stage.

The musical director should make arrangements for the

supply of music stands and lights well in advance of the orchestral rehearsal, and should also make certain that the pit will be arranged in accordance with his wishes.

The two plans which follow show suggested layouts for (*a*) an orchestra of twelve players, including Piano, and (*b*) an orchestra of twenty players, without Piano.

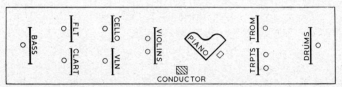

FIG. 19. (*a*). LAYOUT FOR ORCHESTRA OF 12

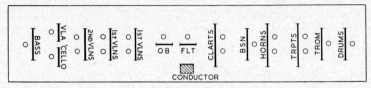

FIG. 19. (*b*). LAYOUT FOR ORCHESTRA OF 20

CUE LIGHTS, ETC.

The musical director should arrange with the stage manager for a cue light to be fixed in the orchestra pit, near the conductor's stand. In professional theatres such a light may, of course, be already provided. Signals (steady light, flashes, etc.) should then be arranged for the start of the Overture, the Opening Chorus, changes of scene, emergencies, etc. In some modern theatres a telephone is provided for the conductor, so that he can be spoken to by the producer or stage manager during the performance. Where no other means of communication exists, a note can be handed in at the door of the orchestra pit, should an emergency arise.

THE MUSICIANS' UNION

When professional musicians are employed, the local representative of the Musicians' Union should be approached, in order that the appropriate rates can be ascertained. Where an existing professional orchestra is taken over, the resident musical director will, of course, be in a position to deal with such matters. During a week of performances, the normal period of orchestral rehearsal allowed for a musical play is a maximum of three hours (including a short break for the musicians); this rehearsal takes place on the day of the first performance. Extra rehearsal time, and rehearsals on other days, must be paid for; higher rates must also be paid for Sunday rehearsals. Where a musician doubles on two instruments, he must, in certain cases, be paid extra; an additional fee is also payable when a musician appears on the stage as well as in the orchestra pit.

CHAPTER TEN

MUSIC AND THE CHORUS

PRINTED vocal scores of most of the well-known light operas and musical plays can be purchased; some of the older scores (especially those of lesser-known musical shows) that are now out of print can be obtained on hire from N.O.D.A. Second-hand sets of vocal scores are often advertised in the N.O.D.A. Bulletin; odd copies may sometimes be obtained from booksellers who specialize in music. (Foyles, Gilbert Stacey, and William Reeves, all in London's Charing Cross Road, usually have a large selection on offer.) In a few cases, only manuscript copies are available, on hire.

Printed vocal scores can sometimes be obtained at a small discount, if ordered in quantity through a local music seller, or from the publishers. Copies will be needed for the singing principals and chorus singers (preferably one copy each), and also for the musical director, chorus master (if any), accompanist, and producer.

THE CONDUCTOR'S SCORE

When the band parts arrive (usually about a month before the show), they will be found to contain, in addition to the orchestral parts, a vocal score for the orchestral pianist, and another for the conductor. Both these scores will (or should) contain word cues, and directions for encores, the rise and fall of the curtain, and so on. In addition, the Conductor's Score will usually be provided with indications of the orchestration.

Sometimes the Conductor's Score and band parts may differ materially from the printed vocal score. The vocal scores of the older musical comedies, for example, have addenda containing certain musical numbers which were added at some time after the original production took place. These are often used in place of, or in addition to, some of the other numbers. It is therefore of the greatest importance that any such alterations should be indicated before rehearsals begin; otherwise rehearsal time may be wasted on music which has been deleted from the show. Where any doubt exists on this point, the musical director should ask the copyright owners (from whom the band parts will be hired) to let him inspect the Conductor's Score in advance, as soon as the show has been booked. He may find that in addition to the alteration of certain numbers, extra music has been added for entrances, exits, dances, etc. He will then be able to make an exact note of all changes in the music, in his own vocal score.

CLASSIFICATION OF VOICES

Music for mixed chorus (i.e. male and female voices) is usually written in four-part harmony—for sopranos, contraltos, tenors, and basses. The approximate compass (which is often exceeded) of these voices is—

There are also two "in-between" voices: the mezzo-soprano, with a compass about a third lower than that of the soprano; and the baritone, with a compass about a third higher than that of the bass. In four-part mixed writing, the mezzo-sopranos sing with the sopranos, and the baritones with the basses. Sometimes one or more of the parts are subdivided, thus increasing the number of real parts. When the soprano voices are divided into two parts, the sopranos sing the upper part, and the mezzo-sopranos the lower; a bass part similarly divided is sung by the baritones and the basses. The number of vocal parts is also reduced on occasions when two or more parts are written in unison.

Music for male voices only is usually written in four parts, both the tenors and the basses being divided into "firsts and seconds." Choral harmony for female voices only is usually written in two parts. It should be noted that whereas music for female voices is always written in the treble clef, either the treble or the bass clefs are used for male voices; and that when the treble clef is used for tenor, baritone, or bass voices, the notes are always written an octave higher than they actually sound.

BALANCE OF VOICES

The size of the chorus in a musical production will depend on the number of suitable singers available, the requirements of the play in question, and the stage dimensions. The ensembles in a full-scale production of *The Vagabond King*, for example, are based on a chorus of thirty-six girls and eighteen men, who with the addition of principals, dancing girls and extras bring the total to eighty-four. In smaller productions these numbers would naturally be scaled down, but assuming that fifty-four chorus singers are used, the balance of voices in a professional production might be somewhat as follows—

20 Sopranos   16 Contraltos   8 Tenors   10 Basses

Strictly from a choral point of view, this disposition of voices is top-heavy, a satisfactory balance being more easily achieved with, say, fifteen Sopranos, twelve Contraltos, twelve Tenors, and fifteen Basses. Such a division of the chorus ensemble would not, however, fulfil the requirements of this particular play, which, from the point of view of stage grouping and visual effect, calls for a chorus of approximately twice as many girls as men.

In practice, the chorus of an amateur musical production is seldom perfectly proportioned. High sopranos, contraltos, and low basses are less plentiful than mezzo-sopranos and baritones, while real tenors, in England at any rate, are rare indeed. The average amateur chorus, therefore, will probably contain too many sopranos (mezzos) and basses (baritones), and too few contraltos and tenors. Good balance must then be obtained by preventing the weaker sections from being overwhelmed by the stronger ones. Perfect balance is especially vital when the voices are unaccompanied (e.g. the madrigal "Bottles" for men's voices, from *Miss Hook of Holland*).

In light opera, Gilbert and Sullivan opera, etc., where the music is of paramount importance, a well-balanced chorus is essential; it is less vital, on the other hand, in musical comedy, pantomime, and revue, where much of the chorus music is sung in unison.

Where one section of the chorus is relatively weak, it is sometimes possible to reinforce it with voices borrowed from another section; if the tenors, for example, find certain passages uncomfortably high, they may often be "helped out" by the contraltos, if they are not otherwise employed; or vice versa.

CHORUS AUDITIONS

Selective auditions to choose the most suitable chorus voices are only possible when an amateur society has a waiting list of prospective members. A new society, or one operating in a sparsely populated district, will probably have no choice but to accept all comers, and to make the best of the material at hand. Whenever possible, however, auditions should be held, since without them it is difficult to secure a high standard of chorus-singing.

Professional chorus auditions are usually held in a theatre, all the applicants being present, and each singing in turn as his or her name is called. Amateurs often find this too great an ordeal, so that it is usually better to hold a private audition for each prospective member, in the presence of a selection committee, including the producer (if available), the musical director, and the accompanist who will play the music presented.

When good part-singing is vital, each applicant should first be asked to sing a song of his or her own choice. Ability to read music at sight is, of course, very desirable, but it is certainly not essential. Of far greater importance is the possession of a fair, normal voice (but not a voice of strident or unpleasant quality, which will fail to blend with the other voices), and a good musical ear. Without the latter, a chorus singer may find it impossible to sustain an inner vocal part. This may not be of great consequence to a soprano, who is usually required to sing the melody. An unmusical contralto, tenor or bass, however, will often be found to be incapable of singing any part *other* than the melody; this cannot fail to influence the other members of the chorus, with the result that accurate part-singing will become an impossibility. A simple ear test is therefore essential. Each applicant should be asked to sing a few single notes, and a simple phrase or two, after these have been played on the Piano by the accompanist or musical director. The degree of ability to do this will give a pretty clear indication whether the applicant will be able to hold his or her own in part-singing.

THE ACCOMPANIST

In amateur societies the accompanist, in addition to playing for the chorus and principals at rehearsals, often plays in the orchestra during performances. Sometimes he also acts as chorus master, though it is seldom advisable for a chorus master to play the Piano himself when taking chorus rehearsals, as he will need to concentrate all his attention on the singing.

The accompanist should be able not only to read Piano music fluently at sight, but also to detect any faults that may occur. A good accompanist can give invaluable help to the musical director, by taking small sectional rehearsals of the chorus and principals, in order to teach them their music.

THE CHORUS MASTER

An efficient chorus master, by training the chorus in the early stages of rehearsal, can relieve the musical director of much of the spade work which he would otherwise be compelled to undertake, thus leaving him free to attend to such matters as the checking of cues, band parts, etc. It is important, however, that there should be the fullest co-operation and understanding between the chorus master and the musical director, so that the latter's ideas regarding choice of *tempo*, expression, style of singing, etc., may be faithfully carried out. A useful partnership can sometimes be formed between a church organist, acting as chorus master, and an orchestral conductor, acting as musical director; the former may have a thorough knowledge of the principles of choral training, but know very little of orchestral technique, whereas the latter is the reverse.

TRAINING THE CHORUS

Methods of chorus training vary, but it will generally be found that the most satisfactory way of tackling a new piece of music will be somewhat as follows—

1. The music should be played through several times at the correct speed by the accompanist, to enable the chorus to grasp the general character of the music. During this playing-through, the chorus should follow their parts from their vocal scores, without singing them.

2. The music should be sung without words, to syllables such

as "tra-la," until both the rhythm and the notes are correctly sung. Unless the members of the chorus are experienced sight-readers, it will be necessary to take each chorus part in turn, the accompanist assisting the particular group of singers concerned, by playing their part prominently on the Piano.

3. The music should next be sung with the words, due regard being paid to proper pronounciation, emphasis, etc.

4. The music and the words being now familiar, attention can be directed to dynamics (*piano, forte, crescendo, diminuendo,* etc.), expression, attack, enunciation, and other points of style and interpretation.

It is of the utmost importance that the chorus trainer (whether chorus master or musical director) should ensure that the chorus follow his beat. Unless any tendency to lag behind, or to race ahead, is firmly checked at the outset, it will quickly develop into a habit. Moreover, such a tendency may become even more pronounced during an actual performance since the orchestra in the theatre is often less easy for the chorus to hear than the Piano in the rehearsal room. Every member of the chorus must therefore be encouraged to watch and follow the beat, and not merely the Piano or some other chorus singer. In actual stage production the chorus should be trained to watch the beat "out of the corner of the eye," so as to avoid giving the impression that their eyes are permanently fixed on the conductor.

By the time the producer is ready to start work on the chorus ensembles, the chorus should be word and note perfect, without reference to the vocal scores. The musical director should not be dismayed, however, when he finds that during the first few production rehearsals the chorus singing deteriorates; on the contrary, he must be content to allow the chorus to concentrate entirely on the stage movements which the producer is teaching them. Once these have been mastered, he will be able to hold further chorus rehearsals to restore the singing to its former standard.

CHORUS LEADERS

When, as sometimes happens, the chorus on the stage cannot all see the beat (some of them may, for example, have their backs to the musical director), one or more chorus leaders must be chosen to take the beat from the musical director and convey it to the other singers. Similarly, when the chorus is singing offstage, suitable sub-conductors should be chosen from those singers who from the wings are able to follow the beat.

BREATHING

Good voice production depends upon deep breathing, i.e. using the full capacity of the lungs, and not merely the upper part. A full breath involves a downward movement of the diaphragm, and an outward movement of the ribs. The body should be comfortably erect, with the chest raised and the shoulders relaxed (i.e. not moving up and down). Before singing, breath can be taken through both the mouth (with the lips slightly opened) and the nose; during singing it will not, of course, be possible to breathe through the nose.

Breath is usually (though by no means invariably) taken at the end of a verbal phrase; in deciding the best places at which to take breath, the meaning of the words should be taken into consideration. Breathing places may be marked by the chorus singers in their vocal scores (lightly in pencil), using the sign √. Continuity of sound in long phrases can be obtained by arranging for small groups of singers to take breath at different points.

ATTACK

To secure a good attack at the start of a phrase, the conductor must ensure that, as he makes the preparatory movement of his baton, the chorus take a good breath. The breath, when taken, should be held momentarily, so that the initial note of the phrase is sung cleanly. It is important that the chorus should "think" their notes before singing them, so that they may attack them at their correct pitch and not, as sometimes happens, scoop up to them. Good attack can be obtained only from a well-rehearsed chorus, who are both confident in themselves, and sure of their notes.

INTONATION

Faulty intonation is usually due to bad voice production. Often the voice is throaty or squeezed out, instead of being produced "forward." Forward production means that the breath is directed well forward in the mouth, the tongue being kept down, and the voice allowed to vibrate in front of the mouth, and in the nasal cavities. The mood of the singers also tends to affect the intonation; a nervous or over-excited chorus is inclined to go sharp, and a bored one flat.

WORDS

A common fault in singing is bad enunciation, with the result that the words are partly or wholly unintelligible to the audience. To obtain clarity of diction, the vowel sounds (upon which one sings) must be pure and undistorted, and the consonants (which merely interrupt the vowel sounds) distinct. Some vowel sounds present little difficulty; others, which are less easy to sing, must be modified slightly in the interests of good tone production. Where such modification is necessary, care must be taken to preserve the integrity of the vowel sound sufficiently for it to be clearly recognized. The different vowels are formed by the modification of the mouth cavity, and by movements of the tongue, lips, and lower jaw. Thus, *ee* and *oo* are formed with the teeth close together, and *ah* with the teeth well apart. For the diphthongs (double vowels, e.g. *ay* as in "day" equals *eh* + *i*), the tongue assumes one vowel position, and then moves to another.

The consonants must neither be omitted (e.g. "Arise zen" for "Arise then"), nor over-articulated (e.g. "The song-uh that-uh I love-uh" for "The song that I love").

Guidance on pronunciation will often have to be given to chorus singers when unusual or foreign words are encountered.

PHRASING, RHYTHM, AND EXPRESSION

Phrasing, in singing, depends both on the shape of the music, and on the words. Some phrases must be sung perfectly *legato*, the notes following one another without a break; other phrases call for *staccato* singing. The chorus must be made to feel the mood of the music (tender, harsh, mysterious, triumphant, etc.), and also to realize where the points of climax occur. *Crescendos* and *diminuendos* must be gradual; most singers invariably begin them too loudly or too softly. Similarly, *rallentandos* and *accelerandos* must not be started too slowly or too quickly.

Amateur choruses (like amateur orchestras) tend to maintain a level tone (a monotonous *mezzo-forte*), and usually have to be coaxed into producing either a real *piano* or a real *forte*. Really soft singing calls for a high degree of breath control, and requires much painstaking rehearsal. Loud singing demands deep breathing, a confident attack, and a complete knowledge of the music.

Lack of rhythm is a common fault which is by no means easy to overcome. It often helps if the words are recited before they are sung, so that points of emphasis and word accentuation may be better appreciated. Accents range from the most delicate pressure in quiet music, to the strongest emphasis (sometimes of every note) in working up to a loud climax.

Characterization and colour play important parts in rhythm and expression. Certain passages call for a breathy tone; others for a harsh or angry one. Excitement can often be portrayed by shouting certain words instead of singing them; and sometimes it is more effective to speak certain words, even though they may be set to music.

Chorus encores should always be prearranged. Variety can sometimes be obtained by having only the melody line sung, and the other parts hummed softly.

CHAPTER ELEVEN

MUSIC AND THE PRINCIPALS

MUCH that has been said in the previous chapter regarding words, phrasing, expression, etc., applies equally to the principals. Certain other points, however, require special consideration.

MUSICAL NUMBERS

In some of the older musical comedies certain musical numbers are usually omitted, and others substituted (see page 106). When vocal scores are given to the principals in advance of the first rehearsals, it is most important that they should be told exactly which numbers are to be included. Otherwise valuable time may be wasted in preparing music which is subsequently left out of the production, and also bad feeling may arise.

In older musical comedies, it may also be necessary to reduce the number of verses and refrains in certain numbers. "Little Miss Wooden Shoes" (*Miss Hook of Holland*), for example, has five verses and refrains—three will usually be found ample for modern requirements. In a number such as this, it is often desirable to repeat part of the music to form a dance (if possible using a different key and orchestration, to avoid monotony), even if this is not indicated in the vocal score. All such alterations must of course be clearly marked in the band parts.

TRANSPOSITIONS

It will sometimes be found that certain songs or concerted numbers in the printed score are too high, or too low, to suit the voices of the performers. It is then necessary for the musical director (in consultation with the singers concerned) to decide what transpositions are desirable, and which are the most suitable keys. Unless the transposition is a simple one, which merely involves a change of key-signature and accidentals (e.g. A Major to A flat Major), it is safer to have the orchestral parts transposed into the new key. Before MS transpositions or orchestrations are made, however, the permission of the copyright owners should be obtained.

TEMPO

In musical comedy the music may, to some extent, be regarded as a series of musical numbers, it being usually possible to withdraw (or alter the position of) one or more of them, without serious damage to the score. The numbers may therefore be treated as separate items, provided that the pace and character of the entire production are maintained.

In Gilbert and Sullivan opera, and other well-written light opera, however, every individual number must be considered in relation to the score as a whole. In conducting light opera, therefore, the musical director must ensure that the *tempi* and phrasing indicated by the composer, are, within reasonable limits, strictly adhered to. Many amateur singers are apt to take their numbers far too slowly, and guidance on suitable *tempi* will often be needed.

Also, many singers have a habit of holding on to high notes; this, if overdone, must be gently but firmly discouraged. Similarly, the practice of introducing pauses other than those indicated by the composer is likely to hold up the flow of the music.

CONCERTED NUMBERS

In rehearsing concerted numbers it will usually be found that those principals who are bad sight-readers, or who cannot read music, will need individual help in learning their parts. It is usually better to let them rehearse their music on their own, aided by the accompanist, until they are note-perfect; the more musical principals will then be free to attend to other matters. Comedians, who are often not particularly musical, sometimes find special difficulty in mastering their parts, and much patient coaching may be necessary.

In concerted numbers, the balance and blend of the voices must be considered; a powerful voice may need to be scaled down to blend with a lighter one, and so on. Important moving parts must be given due prominence, and less important parts subordinated accordingly. A good example of this treatment is the Quartet "In a Contemplative Fashion" (*The Gondoliers*); here the moving parts (in whatever voice they may occur) must be sung *forte* as in the score, while the three other parts are sung *pianissimo*. In concerted singing, unanimity of phrasing, expression, and pronunciation must also receive careful attention.

RECITATIVE

Recitative, or declamation in music, occurs in the Gilbert and Sullivan operas, and in many other light operas and musical plays. It is often taken far too slowly. Though a certain amount of licence is necessary, the rhythm of the words, as *spoken*, should be an approximate guide to the proper speed at which they should be sung.

In conducting recitative, beats during which the orchestra is silent should be indicated very lightly, since a stronger indication might be interpreted by the orchestra as an invitation to play; whereas those beats on (or after) which a chord is to be played must be given firmly.

In certain cases, it is usual to modify the accompaniment to a recitative; for example, a chord which (in the printed score) coincides with the final note of a recitative passage, is often made to follow it. The example below will help to illustrate this point.

I am ac- cur- sed

is usually played thus:

I am ac-cur-sed

ENCORES

In the Gilbert and Sullivan operas the encores are traditional; certain parts of certain numbers are repeated, whereas encores of other numbers are never given. The encores are clearly indicated in the conductor's score which is supplied with each set of band parts. (The conductor's score also contains word cues, and details of the orchestration.)

In other musical shows, encores are generally arranged for certain numbers, to be given if warranted by the applause. It is usually best to let the musical director decide whether or not an encore is to be taken; if he considers that a repetition is justified, he should pick up the musical introduction smartly, before the applause begins to fade. There should always be a clear understanding between the company and the musical director on the question of encores.

When possible, the words—or the style of singing—should be varied for an encore; exact repetitions are apt to be monotonous, though there are exceptions.

CHAPTER TWELVE

THE PRODUCTION STAFF

RETURNING now to the technique of production we are here concerned with those on whom the producer relies for the smooth running of the show.

THE ART DIRECTOR

A keen knowledgeable art director can be of considerable assistance to a society in the selection of its scenery, furniture, costumes, and properties. When a society makes its own scenery and costumes for a production, an art director is almost indispensable.

Although hired costumes for musical shows are as a rule well-designed, colour harmonies can be upset by careless groupings on the stage. The art director can advise on these groupings from the best artistic point of view, and so avoid crude clashes of colour due to incorrect positioning of the artistes wearing the costumes. If modern costumes are obtained locally or supplied by members, the guidance of an art director is invaluable.

He can advise, too, on the most suitable furniture, on the selection or making of historically accurate properties for a period play, and on many other aspects of artistic staging. He can also contribute considerably to the attractive layout and design of the society's publicity matter.

A suitable art director may be found in the nearest Art School, or the art master in one of the local schools might be interested to offer his services to a society. In a small society, or school group, the art director may often act as producer.

THE STAGE MANAGER AND HIS STAFF

On the professional stage, a big musical show will have a stage director in addition to a stage manager and assistants. In an amateur society it is customary to have a stage manager and one or more assistants according to the scale of the production.

It is immaterial whether the person responsible for what happens on the stage is called a stage director or a stage manager. In order to conform with amateur practice and avoid confusion, we will therefore refer to him as the stage manager.

The stage manager is the producer's right-hand man. He must be experienced, dependable, and interested in his job. He is responsible for everything that takes place on the stage, and for all the items concerned with the production—the scenery, effects, lighting, properties, and so on. He is in complete control of the stage staff. As he will have an enormous amount of detail work to supervise, he should have at least one assistant stage manager—A.S.M. for short. The stage manager's work commences with the first rehearsal and continues right through to the final performance of the show, after which he is generally responsible for the return of all material to its various owners.

Before or during the early rehearsals, the stage manager and producer will obtain all the necessary information about the dimensions of the stage and the facilities available for the forthcoming production. They will also decide finally on the scenery, costumes, furniture, properties, additional lighting, etc., so that everything required for the production can be ordered in good time. If the society has appointed an art director, he or she should be brought into any relevant discussions in an advisory capacity.

The stage manager should have done a considerable amount of amateur acting, and be thoroughly familiar with the mechanics of the stage. He should also possess a firm but tactful personality, with plenty of drive, so that he can get his staff to work with him as a team. He can be of enormous help to the producer by taking a load of detail and a lot of worry off his shoulders, leaving him free to concentrate on the creative and artistic side of the production. A show can be ruined by indifferent or incompetent stage management, and it is unfair to a producer to involve him in management detail outside his province.

The stage manager should not play an acting part of any size in the show. He will have quite enough to occupy his time backstage. The show must be kept going, whatever happens. It is his responsibility, and quick decisions are needed to cope with unexpected mishaps, mechanical hold-ups, effects that fail to function, lighting troubles, and a dozen other eventualities. Stage management carries no publicity, no curtain calls, but it can be interesting work to anyone with the aptitude, the knowledge, and the organizing ability to make a success of the job.

In a small society an efficient stage manager is doubly important because he may have to overcome many difficulties which do not arise on a fully-equipped stage. His lighting equipment may be of the most elementary kind. There may be no facilities for flying scenery, and quick changes will present problems. He must, therefore, be a master of improvisation, but in many ways his job will be more of an adventure than that of his more fortunate counterpart working on a theatre stage with the latest equipment.

The A.S.M.

The A.S.M. need not be as experienced as the stage manager. The important qualifications as far as he or she is concerned— many professional A.S.Ms. are women—are enthusiasm and absolute dependability. Very often the A.S.M. is also the prompter.

The stage manager and the A.S.M. are together responsible during the performance for giving the cues from the prompt corner for lighting, effects, scene changes, and bringing the curtain up and down. If the stage manager has to leave the prompt corner the A.S.M. takes charge.

THE PROMPT COPY

During rehearsals the stage manager enters in the libretto all alterations and additions decided on by the producer. This copy of the libretto becomes the official version of the show and is known as the "prompt" copy. The A.S.M. may take over this work at rehearsal when the stage manager is absent on other duties. Later, the cues for lighting, effects, and music will be incorporated in the prompt copy. The prompt copy, in fact, is the stage manager's complete production guide, containing every item of information necessary for the per-formance of the show.

The producer will have his own working copy which should correspond exactly with the stage manager's version. The prompter will use the prompt copy later on in rehearsal when the principals know their lines well enough to dispense with their books.

If the libretto is in manuscript form, the various notes and alterations can be clearly written out on the blank backs of the typewritten pages. The notes thus entered on each blank will refer to the typed page opposite.

If, as is more usually the case, the libretto is in printed form, the best way is to interleave the entire book with blank pages. This can be done in various ways. One is to use a loose-leaf binder slightly larger than the libretto. The printed copy is taken to pieces and the leaves separated. Holes are punched at the backs of the printed pages which are then interleaved with blank pages. The whole combination is then clamped home in its binder. It is a good idea to include a dozen or so blank pages at the end of the prompt copy for miscellaneous notes.

Another method is to use an ordinary note-book, also slightly larger in area than the libretto, and cut out every second page so that about half an inch of it remains in the binding. The libretto is taken to pieces as before and each page pasted or fixed with adhesive tape to the half-inch strips in the book.

In most cases there will be reasonably full stage directions for entrances, exits, and movements already in the libretto. It is the alterations, dialogue changes, and new business introduced by the producer in the course of rehearsal which have to be accurately recorded. These should all be clearly entered on the blank pages, first in pencil and later, when finalized, in ink.

CUES

Cues should be underlined and it is a good idea to use different coloured inks for the purpose, e.g. red for music, blue for lighting, green for effects, and so on. It is also useful to have additional warning cues in advance of the actual cues themselves. These warning cues for ensembles, finales, effects, lighting and scene changes, blackouts, and other items—can be entered on the blank pages facing the dialogue in bold panels. For example,

| CHORUS | AEROPLANE |

| BLACKOUT | QUICK CHANGE |

| SUNSET EFFECTS | CURTAIN |

| FINALE ACT 1 | EXPLOSION |

This system of warning cues in advance of actual cues provides a series of useful signposts, which enable the producer and stage manager to anticipate complicated moves and changes in the later stages of rehearsal, as well as during the actual performance. It should not be applied to normal cues, but only to items presenting special difficulty and for which advance warning would be useful.

WORKING PLOTS

Among the stage manager's responsibilities is the preparation of the following records—

> A scene plot
> A property and furniture plot
> An effects plot
> A costume plot
> A lighting plot

As a rule these are contained in most libretti, based on the original productions, and it is possible that, in consultation with the producer, they will have to be modified for amateur purposes, especially in respect of lighting and scenery.

The Scene Plot[1]

The scene plot consists of a series of ground plans of the sets, showing how the flats, backings, cloths, rostrums, staircases, doors, furniture, and other items are arranged. The scene plot should be on view at rehearsals. During the show it should be posted up for reference by the stage staff. A copy

[1] See page 144.

PROPERTY AND FURNITURE PLOT

(By permission of Samuel French, Ltd.)

Act I, Scene I

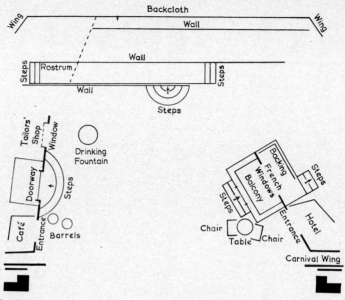

On Stage—

    Café table. *On it:* Chianti bottle, glasses as required.

    2 chairs.

    2 small wine barrels.

    On balcony rail: rug.

    Under balcony: baskets of flowers, baskets of fruit.

    On barrels: Chianti bottle, glasses as required.

Off Stage—

    Properties for CHORUS: basket of washing, shopping baskets, Gondo-liers' poles, pole with onions, duster for waiter, bunches of flowers.

    Tray. *On it:* cutlery (PIETRO).

    Towel (PAOLO).

    Baskets of flowers (FLOWER SELLERS).

    Trays with postcards, scarves, fruit, etc. (VENDORS).

    Tray. *On it:* 2 glasses of wine (PIETRO).

    Newspaper (CHORUS MAN).

    Luggage (POLEIGH).

    Telephone instrument on long cord (POLEIGH).

    Telephone receiver on long cord (PAOLO).

Personal—

    TESTI: visiting card, roll of notes.

    POLEIGH: monocle.

    MAGGIE: handbag. *In it:* cablegram.

    EDITH: handbag. *In it:* letters, phial of perfume.

    LISA: gloves.

should be bound up in the prompt book, and in the producer's libretto, if not already included.

The Property Master

The property master is responsible for all the furniture and properties used in the show. When the scenes are set at dress rehearsal he marks the positions of all furniture and other pieces on the stage for each scene, so that everything will be in exactly the same place at every performance. He also arranges the properties near the entrances at each side of the stage, so that they are most conveniently placed for getting them on and off. Small articles are put on tables near the entrances. He must keep a close check on every item; small props have a curious tendency to disappear.

The players usually look after their own personal properties such as walking-sticks, spectacles, snuff-boxes, and so on, but the property master remains responsible for checking them at all performances to make sure they are all available when required.

The Property and Furniture Plot

This consists of a complete list of all furniture and properties used in the show. Copies of the plot will be required by the stage manager, the A.S.M., the producer, and the property master. It should be incorporated in the prompt book and displayed for reference in the prompt corner during the show.

If the property plot is a long and detailed one, it is often advisable to list the articles required for stage entrances R and L in two columns for easier reference.

The Effects Plot

The effects plot records all the visual and sound effects produced mechanically off-stage as distinct from those controlled by the players on the stage. A thunderstorm, with lightning, is an example of combined visual and sound effects produced off-stage by means of a record, or with a thunder sheet, used in conjunction with floods switched quickly on and off. Effective sound records are obtainable from the leading gramophone companies and should be played on suitable sound equipment of adequate volume.

GAY ROMANCE

Effects Plot

Act I, Scene 1

Cue 1.	After Overture, on Rise of Curtain.	FAIRGROUND EFFECTS, CROWD NOISES (Records).
Cue 2.	DAISY. ". . . don't spoil the party!"	BICYCLE BELL.
Cue 3.	After Exit of Count, Baron and Chauffeurs.	MOTOR CAR MOVING OFF (Record).

Act II, Scene 3

Cue 4.	SERVANT. "Very good, Your Excellency."	CHURCH BELLS. CHEERING CROWDS (Records).

Act II, Scene 4

Cue 5.	COLONEL. "Good luck to you, Your Highness."	AIRCRAFT STARTING UP (Record).
Cue 6.	After Exit of Elga and Soldiers during Reprise of "The Call to Arms."	AIRCRAFT PASSING OVERHEAD and AWAY. CHEERING CROWDS (Records).

The Costume Plot

The costume plot is simply a detailed list, grouped under the headings "Men's Costumes" and "Women's Costumes," scene by scene, of what all the characters and the chorus wear throughout the show. Sometimes costume plots are not included in the libretti of certain shows, especially when modern dress is worn, and a complete list should be compiled by the producer and stage manager as soon as possible, as some of the costumes and dresses may have to be obtained from more than one source.

The costume plot should be incorporated, when completed, in the prompt copy and producer's copy. The wardrobe mistress and wardrobe master should be supplied with details as early as possible during the rehearsal period, so that any costumes which cannot be hired in the ordinary way may be made or purchased in good time. The costume plot should include stockings, socks, shirts, collars, ties, boots and shoes, and any other necessary items. Guests in a fashionable wedding scene have been known to turn up at the dress rehearsal wearing brown shoes and sports socks when these details have been overlooked in the costume plot. Some plots are incomplete in this respect and any details which have been omitted should be added as soon as possible. It is also advisable to check all items with the hiring contractors when ordering.

THE DESERT SONG

COSTUME PLOT

(By permission of Samuel French, Ltd.)

MEN

PIERRE. *Act I, Scene* 1. RED SHADOW costume consisting of riding-boots, red quick-change trousers, red tunic and broad belt to match. Red head-dress and mask to slip up and down like a visor. Red cloak.

Act I, Scene 3. RED SHADOW costume as above. Riding-kit consisting of riding-boots, cord breeches, white shirt, collar and tie, brown tweed coat.

Act II, Scene 1. RED SHADOW costume as above.

Act II, Scene 3. RED SHADOW costume as above. Riding kit as above.

Act II, Scene 4. RED SHADOW costume as above.

Act II, Scene 5. Riding-kit as above. RED SHADOW cloak, head-dress and mask.

SID EL KAR. *Throughout.* Riff tunic costume with belt and riding-boots. Turban.

HADJI. *Act I, Scene* 1. Riff peasant costume —djeelaba and turban.

HASSI. *Throughout.* Riff tunic costume with belt and riding-boots. Turban.

MINDAR. *Throughout.* Riff costume as chorus.

BENJAMIN. *Throughout.* Grey lounge suit.

In Act II, Scene 1 he puts on a large white djeelaba which has an enormous red star and crescent embroidered on it back and front.

In Act II, Scene 2, he has a replica of Susan's "Semi" frock with her hat.

PAUL. *Throughout.* French Captain's uniform of the Foreign Legion.

BIRABEAU. *Throughout.* French General's uniform of the Foreign Legion.

ALI BEN ALI. *Act II, Scenes* 1 *and* 3. White Riff costume with broad belt and turban. Red morocco shoes.

LA VERGNE. *Throughout.* French Lieutenant's uniform of the Foreign Legion.

DE BOUSSAC. *Throughout.* French Sergeant's uniform of the Foreign Legion.

THE MALE CHORUS throughout alternate between Soldiers of the Foreign Legion and Riffs. As the latter, they wear long djeelabas, and turbans. The boots are doubled. In their last entrance as Soldiers they use white cap-covers. The servants wear white djeelabas and fezzes. The guards wear green tunics, white baggy trousers, red morocco shoes, and turbans.

WOMEN

MARGOT. *Act I, Scene* 3. French Officer. Evening dress. Riding habit.

Act II, Scene 1. Riding-habit from Act I. Scene 1 (without coat).

Act II, Scene 3. Harem costume.

Act II, Scene 5. Summer afternoon frock.

SUSAN. *Act I, Scene* 2. Evening dress.

Act I, Scene 3. "Semi" frock (suitable for "IT" number).

Act II, Scene 1. As Act I, Scene 3.

Act II, Scene 2. Wears Benjamin's white djeelaba.

Act II, Scene 5. As Act I, Scene 3.

EDITH. *Act I, Scene* 2. Evening dress as Singing Chorus.

AZURI. *Act I, Scene* 1. Native costume.

Act I, Scene 3. As Act I, Scene 1. Native dancing costume.

Act II, Scene 3. Native dancing costume as above with shawl.

Act II, Scene 5. Native dancing costume.

CLEMENTINA. *Act II, Scene* 1. Spanish dancer's costume.

NERI. *Act I, Scene* 1. Riff peasant woman.

THE SINGING CHORUS wear evening dress throughout Act 1, Scene 3, long Spanish dresses in Act II, Scene 1, and afternoon frocks in Act II, Scene 5.

THE DANCING CHORUS wear French soldiers' costumes in Act I, Scene 3, then change to evening frocks (suitable for dancing). Eight of them change into Azuri Dancer costumes for finale.

For Act II, Scene 1, they wear short Spanish costumes, and for Act II, Scene 5, they wear afternoon frocks, changing if possible into their French soldiers' uniforms for the calls.

The Wardrobe

For a heavy musical show with a large chorus involving several costume changes, it is necessary to have a wardrobe mistress to look after the women's dresses, and a wardrobe master to be responsible for the men's costumes. They will require assistants who can also lend a hand as dressers. The wardrobe staff are responsible to the stage manager for checking in all the costumes, making final adjustments for exact fitting, and for their care and maintenance during the run of the show.

A workroom should be set aside for the wardrobe department for carrying out repairs, ironing, and cleaning, so that the costumes will preserve their smart appearance at every performance.

Make-up and Hairdressing

It is usual, in the case of a big show, for the society to employ one or more make-up artists and a hairdresser. Not many amateurs can make themselves up properly for the stage, and professional help is desirable. Women's hair styles require expert attention if the show is to look right from the front. The employment of experts in these two departments is money well spent.

A word about wigs. They should be worn only if the period demands them. Very often money is spent unnecessarily on the hire of wigs when the same effect can be obtained with the natural hair, or by the addition of false pieces which the local hairdresser can supply. Or, for example, if headgear is worn which completely covers the head, the wearing of wigs underneath is superfluous. The hairdresser should be consulted before any wigs are ordered.

Crêpe hair should be used with discretion, and on no account should false beards fitted on wire be used for any serious make-up.

The Lighting Plot

The lighting plot should be worked out as far as possible before production, and supplied to the electrician in good time before dress rehearsal. A full lighting plot is usually included in the libretti of most musical plays. It is very often the plot used in the original professional production, and may demand more elaborate equipment than is found in most provincial theatres and halls. It provides a useful guide, however, for the preparation of a more modified plot to conform with whatever facilities are available. It will not be possible to complete the lighting plot until the producer sees the scenery set up on the stage. The lighting rehearsal is usually arranged on the afternoon preceding the opening performance. The following extract, by permission of Samuel French, Ltd., from the lighting plot of *Magyar Melody* is a typical example.

LIGHTING PLOT

NOTE ON LIGHTING

The Lighting Plot is based on circuits in Floats and Battens of No. 18 Blue, No. 51 Gold and No. 7 Rose [or No. 12 if preferred]. The F.O.H. lighting is based on four circuits, No. 36 Lavender, No. 8 Salmon, No. 51 Gold and No. 7 Light Rose. If only three circuits can be arranged in the F.O.H., the No. 51 Gold may be eliminated, and cues for this colour may be covered with No. 8 Salmon.

If the colour media in the installation are materially deeper than the above, a white circuit may be found advisable when exceptional brightness is desired by the Producer.

ACT I

At cue from Orchestra. Floats: Pink, Gold and Blue, $\frac{1}{2}$.

2nd cue from Orchestra. House lights out.

3rd cue from Orchestra. Floats up [as below] as curtain rises.

1. *To open* . . .
   Floats: Pink, Gold, Blue, full.
   Nos. 1, 2, and 3 Battens: Pink, Gold, Blue, full.
   No. 4 Batten: Blue and Pink only, full.
   No. 1 Spot Bar: Acting Area c., No. 51 Gold.
                   Acting Areas R.C. and L.C., No. 8 Salmon.
   No. 2 Spot Bar: Acting Area up c., No. 36 Lavender.
                   Acting Areas up R.C. and up L.C., No. 51 Gold.
   Flood cloth No. 17 Steel and Frost.
   No. 4 Amber lengths in farmhouse R.
   Blue lengths on Barn backing L.
   F.O.H. flood No. 8 Salmon and No. 51 Gold.

2. *Cue.* During the final bars of the Opening Number, slowly fade in No. 36 Lavender Spot from No. 2 Bar on wall plaque.

3. *Cue. As Limes pick up* JULIKA:
   Fade out F.O.H.

4. *Cue. As Limes fade at end of song:*
   Fade in F.O.H.

5. *Cue. As* MICHAEL *sings:*
   Fade out F.O.H., and Spot on plaque.

6. *Cue. As* MICHAEL *exits, and Limes fade out:*
   Fade in F.O.H.

7. *Cue. As Limes pick up* ROSZI:
   Fade out No. 8 Salmon in F.O.H. only.

8. *Cue.* *As Limes change on* MICHAEL:
    Fade out No. 51 Gold in F.O.H.

9. *Cue.* *At end of duet, as the* DANCERS *enter and Limes fade:*
    Fade in F.O.H. No. 8 Salmon, No. 51 Gold and No. 36 Lavender.

10. *Cue.* *As the* DANCERS *exit:*
    Fade out No. 36 Lavender in F.O.H.

11. *Cue.* *As Limes pick up* JULIKA *and* MIKKI:
    Fade out F.O.H.

12. *Cue.* *As Limes pick up* DANCERS:
    Fade No. 51 Gold in Floats and Battens.

13. *Cue.* *As Limes fade out at end of Czardas:*
    Fade in No. 51 Gold in Floats and Battens, and follow with fade in
    of F.O.H. No. 8 Salmon and No. 51 Gold.

14. *Cue.* *As Limes pick up the* EMPRESS:
    Fade out No. 51 Gold in F.O.H.

15. *Cue.* *As Limes fade on the exit of the* EMPRESS:
    Fade in No. 51 Gold in F.O.H.

16. *Cue.* *As Limes pick up* ROSZI:
    Fade out No. 51 Gold in F.O.H.

LIMES PLOT

[*The following are the cues for focus spots on* PRINCIPALS *for numbers, and occasionally during dialogue. Against each cue is indicated the colour medium most suitable to the character and the moment.*]

ACT I

Cue 1. Follow MAYOR. [No. 51 Gold.]

Cue 2. MAYOR. ". . . *while I look for my hat.*"—OFF.

Cue 3. For No. 2. Follow JULIKA [No. 36 Lavender.]

Cue 4. At end of Number—OFF.

Cue 5. At entrance of MICHAEL, spot and follow. [No. 51 Gold.]

Cue 6. At exit of MICHAEL—OFF.

Cue 7. At entrance of ROSZI, spot and follow, to cover JULIKA. [No. 36 Lavender.]

Cue 8. At entrance of MICHAEL, spot and follow. [No. 51 Gold.]

Cue 9. For No. 5. Change spot on MICHAEL to No. 36 Lavender and follow.

Cue 10. At end of Number, as ROSZI and MICHAEL go up stage—OFF.

Cue 11. For No. 6. Follow JULIKA and MIKKI. [No. 36 Lavender.]

Cue 12. At exit of MIKKI and JULIKA at end of Number. Spot and follow DANCERS. [Colours as desired.]

Cue 13. At end of Czardas Ballet—OFF.

Cue 14. At entrance of EMPRESS. Follow EMPRESS. [No. 8 Salmon.]

Cue 15. At entrance of MICHAEL, follow throughout scene, covering ROSZI on her entrance also. [No. 51 Gold.]

Cue 16. At exit of EMPRESS. Fade out spots in Cues 14 and 15.

Cue 17. At entrance of ROSZI, follow her to exit, then—OFF. [No. 36 Lavender.]

The Electrician

If the production is in a theatre, there will be a permanent electrician on the stage staff. If the society has to supply its own electrician, he should be an experienced technician who understands the mechanics of stage lighting. He will require assistants according to the equipment on the stage and in the front of the house.

In small halls where stage lighting equipment is scanty or non-existent the position is different. The society's producer, or stage manager, will have to devise simple lighting equipment of his own. The local electrician can be useful in this connexion. He will probably be glad to suggest ways and means of meeting the shortcomings without undue expense. The lighting plot of the show may have to be drastically modified, but effective results can still be achieved with comparatively simple equipment.

The Stage Carpenter

The stage carpenter is the stage handyman. He is responsible to the stage manager for the smooth operation of the scenery and for maintaining it in good condition. He rehearses the setting of each scene, and, when approved by the producer, marks all cloths and flats in their proper order for the show before striking the sets.

The Prompter

A prompter is essential. Sometimes this work is undertaken by the A.S.M. but many societies prefer to appoint someone to do the job exclusively. Whoever does it should commence work when the principals know their lines well enough to dispense with their scripts.

The prompter must be resourceful. Sometimes he has to decide quickly during a show which cue to give in order to cover up an awkward moment when two, not one, characters "dry up." Prompting can be successfully done by women, as they often possess the right pitch of voice, just sufficient to penetrate to the stage but not to the audience.

The Call Boy

The call boy need not, of course, be a boy at all. The duties can be taken by any reliable member of the society. Under the direction of the stage manager, it is the call boy's duty to warn the company half an hour before the curtain is due to rise. A second warning is given by the call boy fifteen minutes later, and five minutes before the curtain rises the final call for beginners is made. He is also responsible from the beginning to the end of the show for warning artistes to stand by when they are due to appear on the stage.

IMPROVISATION

We have dealt in this chapter with the normal stage staff necessary for the average operatic production. Whether the society be large or small the duties described should be covered, and staff allocated according to conditions and the scale of the production. Obviously on a small stage there will not be room for a large production staff and some improvisation will be necessary to obtain reasonable results with limited resources. It is better to make bold revisions to scenery, property, costume, and lighting plots in order to simplify production than to attempt the impossible. How a small stage with limited facilities can be used to the best advantage is described in a later chapter.

CHAPTER THIRTEEN

THE THEATRE STAGE

IT is important that the aspiring producer and stage manager should understand the mechanics and operation of the modern theatre stage.

THE STAGE

Although many of the large operatic societies are fortunate enough to be able to present their shows on theatre stages, the majority of the smaller societies are denied this advantage. There are excellent stages in many halls and cinemas which, although their construction does not permit scenery to be "flown," i.e. raised and lowered mechanically as required, are nevertheless provided with first-class lighting and other equipment. Smaller stages with more limited facilities present problems for the producer. A working knowledge of the modern theatre stage will, however, be of value in getting the best out of what equipment there is, and in supplementing it effectively.

Proscenium

The proscenium is the frame or arch through which the audience sees the show. Beyond the proscenium is that part of the theatre known as "backstage." Here will be found the scene dock, workshops, offices, dressing rooms, and the mechanical and lighting equipment required for presenting a show. The rest of the theatre, apart from backstage, is known as the front of the house, which is connected to the stage by a fireproof pass-door.

False Proscenium

This is a smaller proscenium within the main stage proscenium. It consists of a flat at each side of the stage and a framed border. With a false proscenium small scenes can be played in front while larger scenes are being set behind. A small scene set inside a larger one is known as an "inset."

Apron

The Apron is the part of the stage which extends beyond the front curtain, or "act drop," as it is sometimes called. In Elizabethan times the apron was important to the action, and formed a "forestage" which extended well forward into the auditorium so that the players had their audience on three sides. Few modern theatres have aprons and where they do exist they are usually quite shallow.

Floats

The floats, or footlights, occupy the portion of the stage in front of the curtain, and are sunk into the stage out of view of the audience.

Safety Curtain

This is a fireproof curtain, made of steel and asbestos, which cuts off the stage from the auditorium in case of fire. It must be lowered in view of the audience once during each performance to ensure that it is in working order.

Front Curtain

The front curtain operates immediately behind the safety curtain. It can either be a canvas painted cloth or, as is more usual, heavy curtains or tabs which can be flown.

Rake

Many stages are constructed so that they slope downwards towards the audience. This slope is known as a "rake." Its purpose is to give depth to the scene from the audience's viewpoint. Without a rake the scene would lack perspective, with the characters moving about the stage in a flat plane. The carpet in a room interior, for example, would not be visible from the stalls level if there were no rake. Exterior scenes would lose much of their atmosphere and composition with no visible "ground," giving the effect of a picture which has been cut off at the bottom. In some theatres the stage is constructed without a rake, the auditorium being adequately sloped instead. The object is the same, to give the audience a better view of the scene.

Acting Area

The acting area is that part of the stage enclosed by the scenery where the action of the show as seen by the audience takes place.

Setting Line

This is the line down-stage towards the proscenium up to which the scenery is set. The position of the setting line is, as a rule, governed by the position of No. 1 lighting batten and the spot bar.

Spot Bar

The spot bar is a fixed metal rod extending across the stage, usually in front of No. 1 lighting batten. A series of spot lights, frequently twelve in number, are clamped to the spot bar in the necessary positions for directional lighting.

Carpet Cut

The carpet cut is a long narrow strip of hinged wood running along the stage at the setting line, or just behind the front curtain. Its purpose is to allow the front edge of stage cloths to be inserted and trapped, i.e. clamped down flush with the stage by means of the hinged strip, instead of nailing them down.

Traps

A trap is a hole cut in the stage floor to enable action to take place below stage level, e.g. the grave-digger scene in *Hamlet*. Traps are also used when characters have to make an entrance from a lower level, up a slope or up a flight of stairs, e.g. Mr. Hook's entrance from the cellar in *Miss Hook of Holland*.

The mechanical star trap, operated by counterweights, was a feature of the spectacular pantomimes of the Edwardian era. It is rarely used to-day.

Cyclorama

This is the term given to a canvas structure set in the form of a curve round the sides and back of the stage to represent sky. The cyclorama is used in place of a backcloth or skycloth, and is particularly effective with simple scenery consisting of groundrows and built-up rostrums.

A permanent cyclorama, made of plaster and timber and shaped like the section of a large dome, with special lighting set in a cyclorama pit to conceal the lamps from view, is a feature of some theatre stages.

SCENERY

The average theatre stage contains two main types of equipment: mechanical equipment for operating the scenery; and electrical equipment for lighting it.

Two types of scenery have to be dealt with—

1. Scenery which is hung from horizontal lengths of timber or tubular metal, known as battens,[1] from above.
2. Scenery which stands with support on the stage itself.

The mechanical equipment for moving the scenery is mainly concerned with scenery suspended from a structure in the roof known as the "grid."

Grid

The average theatre stage is usually just over twice as high as the scenery, to enable it to be flown.

Over the stage, high up in the roof, is the grid, a network of timber or steel joists, to which is fixed a series of blocks and pulleys. Through these pass ropes known as "lines" which, when operated, move the scenery up and down as required.

KEY TO FIG. 20

1. Carpet Cut.	10. Prompt Side.
2. Fly Galleries.	11. O.P. Side.
3. Switchboard.	12. Acting Area.
4. Proscenium Wings and Tormentors.	13. Electrical Dips.
5. Spot Bar.	14. Front Curtain.
6. Proscenium Border.	15. Safety Curtain.
7. Floats.	16. Grid.
8. Setting Line.	17. Scenery Packs.
9. Stage Manager's Desk and Cue Board.	18. Sets of Lines.

Cloths, borders, lighting battens, etc. (not included in this diagram) are suspended from the grid on three lines in the same manner as the safety curtain, front curtain, and spot bar.

[1] The term "batten" is also applied to a row of lights similarly suspended above the stage.

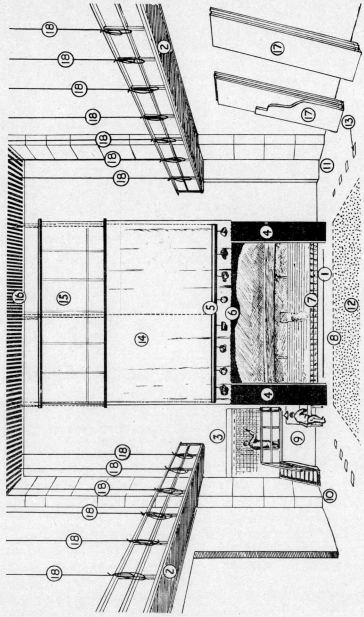

Fig. 20. Skeleton Plan of Theatre Stage from behind the Proscenium, facing the Audience

(Key on opposite page)

Lines

There are three lines to every set. Each set of three lines is used to deal with whatever is hung on any batten. On a cloth, for example, or on a border, two of the lines are attached to each end of the batten with the third line in the centre.

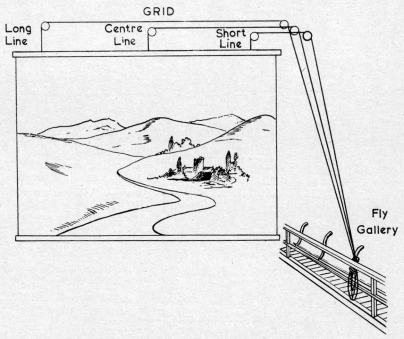

FIG. 21. A BACKCLOTH HUNG ON A SET OF LINES
The three lines are secured to a cleat on the rail of the fly gallery.

The lines are run across and over the pulleys to the fly gallery at the side of the stage. Some theatres have one fly gallery, others have two, one on each side of the stage.

The lines are looped round iron fixtures on the fly gallery. These are larger editions of the cleats on the backs of flats.

The lines vary in length with their distance from the fly gallery to the batten, and for this reason are called short, centre, and long, the short line being on the working side.

These terms are used when a cloth, border or other item suspended on a batten is being adjusted for height and level. When the correct level and height have been arrived at, the cloths, borders, etc., are said to be "deaded." The flyman is instructed to raise or lower the short, centre, and long lines until the desired result is obtained.

The stage staff operating the machinery for flying the scenery usually work on the O.P. side of the stage, i.e. stage right. (O.P. is a contraction for "opposite prompt," the prompt side, or P.S. for short, being on stage left.)

Counterweights

Heavy scenery may take more than one man to pull it away unless the stage is equipped with a counterweight system. Here, weights provide a compensating balance, the short, centre and long lines being controlled by an endless rope so the heavy load can be manipulated by one man. The number of flymen and other stage staff required to handle all the scenery will, of course, vary according to the size and nature of the production.

Scenery which is hung on battens from above the stage includes—

Cloths

This term is applied to draperies and painted canvas used as a backcloth, frontcloth, sky-cloth, cut-cloth, or backing. A cut-cloth is a cloth in which, for example, an entrance has been cut to conform with the design and so make it practical.

A French flat is a framed cloth which contains practical doors, windows, or other features of design which require it to be rigid.

Borders

These consist of material, either canvas painted to represent foliage, sky, ceilings, etc., or draped material, according to the nature of the scene. Borders serve to mask the upper part of the stage, and they also screen the lights suspended on the light battens behind them. Borders are identified when setting a scene as No. 1 Border, No. 2 Border, and so on, starting from the proscenium.

The battens carrying the lights behind the borders are similarly numbered—No. 1 Lighting Batten, No. 2 Lighting Batten, etc.

Cut-tail Borders and Headers

Cut-tail borders are cut-out pieces of scenery used in conjunction with ground-set pieces to form a complete unit, e.g. the branches and foliage of a tree and its trunk. The trunk stands supported on the stage, and the cut-tail border of foliage is lowered into position from above to form the complete tree. Headers are framed pieces of scenery suspended from above to complete, for example, an arched structure. Flats form the support—it might be a set of pillars—and the header, when lowered into position, might complete a series of arches.

Gauzes

When a scene is painted on a gauze or fine net cloth and lit from the front, it appears exactly the same as an ordinary painted canvas cloth. When the front lighting is dimmed out, and bright lighting brought in behind, the gauze becomes transparent. The scene on the gauze melts away and the scene behind predominates. When this effect has been achieved the gauze is usually flown, leaving the new scene entirely clear. Gauzes are used for flashback scenes or purely for effect.

Tabs

These consist of any pair of curtains which open and close when operated on runners on a tab rail. Some tabs can also be pulled up, and to the sides, to form a festoon border effect. Some can be flown in addition, thus making three effects available as required. This type is frequently used for the front curtain. The term "tab" is an abbreviation of the word "tableau."

Scenery which stands with support on the stage includes—

Flats

A flat is a piece of painted canvas stretched over a wooden frame. The walls of a room on the stage are built up from flats temporarily fastened together to form a box set.

Flats vary in size from three to eight feet wide by twelve to eighteen feet high, and are fastened together on the stage by means of lines and cleats. The line from one flat is passed over the cleat in the next flat and secured.

Flats are supported by extension braces fitted with a hook which engages a screw-eye in the flat. The other end of the brace is held in position by a stage screw or brace weight. Brace weights are to be preferred as they do not damage the stage.

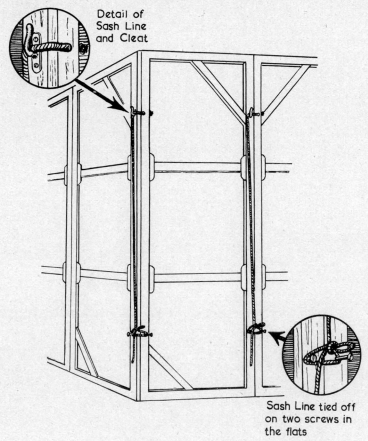

Detail of
Sash Line
and Cleat

Sash Line tied off
on two screws in
the flats

FIG. 22. FLATS, SHOWING CLEATS, LINES, AND TIE-OFFS

Flat Units

Two flats hinged together to form one complete unit are known as a two-fold; three flats similarly hinged, a three-fold.

When two or more flats are secured rigidly together by nailing wooden battens along the back, they are said to be "battened out."

As flying is the quickest method of moving scenery, flats battened out to form the back wall of a set, for example, are often flown to save time and labour.

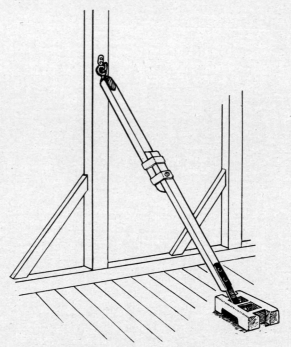

FIG. 23. FLAT SUPPORTED BY WOODEN EXTENSION BRACE HELD IN POSITION BY BRACE WEIGHT

Wings

These are flats set at an angle on each side of the stage and used for entrances and exits. The sides of the stage outside the acting area are also known as wings. A French flat used as a wing is called a French wing.

Tormentors

These are flats placed on each side of the proscenium at right angles to it. The purpose of tormentors is to mask the prompt and O.P. sides just behind the proscenium, and the actors' entrances and exits down-stage.

Returns

Returns are movable flats, usually painted black, used to mask in the prompt and O.P. corners in the absence of tormentors. They also form a frame for the setting. The last two flats of a set running on and off stage, used to mask in, are also called returns.

Backings

Backings are pieces of scenery—they can be either flats or cloths—placed behind doors, windows, and other openings.

Reveal

This is a flat or other piece of scenery placed at right angles to an opening to show thickness or depth.

Groundrows and Cut-outs

Low pieces of scenery representing objects like exterior walls, trees, hedges, distant landscapes, etc. The term "groundrow" is also applied to footlights used behind a scenic groundrow or cut-out, to illuminate the lower part of a backing.

Packs

Packs of scenery are groups of flats and other units stacked at the sides or back of the stage in their correct order for setting up the various scenes as conveniently and speedily as possible. A pack yet to be used for a forthcoming scene is called a *live* pack; one which has already been used and is no longer required during the show is known as a *dead* pack.

Rostrum

A platform of wood used for raised terraces, stairs, etc. It can be of varying height with one or more steps, or treads, placed in front to form a staircase.

Truck

A truck is a low rostrum mounted on castors, and on it may be constructed scenery to represent, for example, a house or impressive entrance to a large building. Trucks can be quickly wheeled away and are also used to carry complete scenes when a rapid change is required.

Stage Cloth

A canvas floor covering for the stage painted to suit the scene, e.g. a carpet, tiled floor, or other interior design; or, in the case of an exterior scene, a lawn, paved courtyard, etc.

A SCENE PLOT IN DETAIL

The following Scene Plot from *Bless the Bride* illustrates many of the types of scenery which have been described in this chapter. The ground plans should be studied in conjunction with the photographs of the scenes as they appear on the stage.

BLESS THE BRIDE

Synopsis of Scenes

ACT I

Scene 1: The Grange, Mayfield—The Lawn. July, 1870.

Scene 2: The Grange, Mayfield—A Shrubbery. (Front Scene.)

Scene 3: The Grange, Mayfield—The Hall.

Scene 4: Lucy's Nursery. (Inset.)

Scene 5: The Hall (Same as Scene 3).

ACT II

Scene 1: La Plage, Eauville.

Scene 2: A Street, Eauville (Front Scene).

Scene 3: The Café des Pommes, Eauville.

Scene 4: The Grange, Mayfield. March, 1871 (Gauze).

Scene 5: The Grange, Mayfield—The Hall. (Same as Act I, Scene 3.)

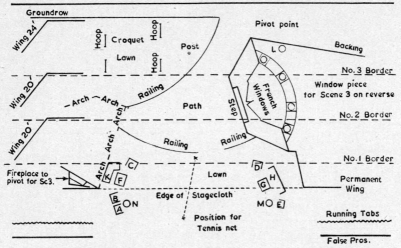

FIG. 24. GROUND PLAN OF ACT I, SCENE I. THE GRANGE,
THE LAWN

A, B, C, D, E. Bamboo chairs. *K.* Garden seat.
F, G. White wicker tables. *L.* Gilt pedestal, vase, flowers.
H. White wicker settee. *M, N.* Wooden stools.

Set on Lawn. 4 croquet hoops, 4 croquet balls, 14 croquet mallets.

Note the truck set for the French windows which swings round and forms the
window piece for Scene 3 on reverse. Similarly, the Fireplace down R. swings
into position when required for Scene 3.

(By courtesy of Samuel French, Ltd.)

Denis de Marne

FIG. 25. ACT I, SCENE I. THE GRANGE, THE LAWN
(By courtesy of Samuel French, Ltd.)

145

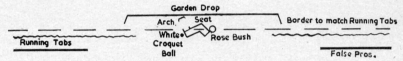

FIG. 26. GARDEN DROP AND SETTING FOR ACT I, SCENE 2.
THE GRANGE, A SHRUBBERY
(By courtesy of Samuel French, Ltd.)

Denis de Marney

FIG. 27. ACT I, SCENE 2. THE GRANGE, A SHRUBBERY
(By courtesy of Samuel French, Ltd.)

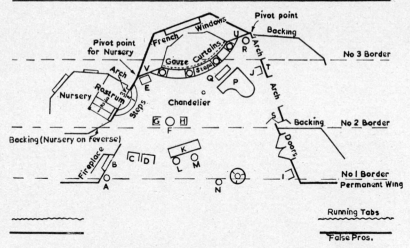

FIG. 28. GROUND PLAN OF ACT I, SCENE 3. THE GRANGE, THE HALL

A. Fire screen. *B.* Fireplace. *C.* Small armchair. *D.* Wing armchair. *E.* Black work table. *F.* Chess table, board and chess men. *G, H, I, J.* Chairs. *K.* Regency table (head to P.S.). *L.* Low beaded footstool. *M.* Low gilt stool. *N.* Bamboo stool. *O.* Conversation seat. *P.* Piano. *Q.* Duet stool. *R.* Gilt pedestal, vase, flowers. *S.* Four-fold screen. *T, U, V.* Gilt three-branch candle brackets.

Note that the French window truck set in Act I, Scene 1 has been swung into reverse to form the pillared rostrum and steps to the window for this scene. The fireplace has also been moved into position from Act I, Scene 1. The rostrum and steps R. also swing round to use in reverse for the Nursery Scene, Act I, Scene 4.

(By courtesy of Samuel French, Ltd.)

Denis de Marney

FIG. 29. ACT I, SCENE 3. THE GRANGE, THE HALL
(By courtesy of Samuel French, Ltd.)

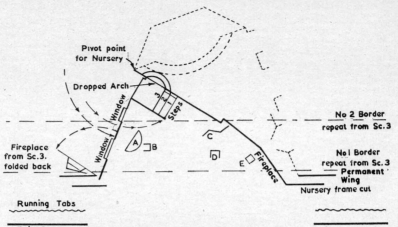

FIG. 30. GROUND PLAN OF ACT I, SCENE 4. THE GRANGE,
LUCY'S NURSERY

A. Dressing table. *B.* Cane chair. *C.* Bamboo three-fold scrap screen. *D.* Cane armchair. *E.* Stool. The rostrum and steps in Scene 3 are now swung round to reverse for this scene. The fireplace has been swung back and window flats set in front at R. The large truck set has also been cleared. This type of scene is called an inset. In this case it is triangular in shape.

(By courtesy of Samuel French, Ltd.)

Denis de Marney

FIG. 31. ACT I, SCENE 4. THE GRANGE, LUCY'S NURSERY
(By courtesy of Samuel French, Ltd.)

Act I, Scene 5 is the same as Scene 3

148

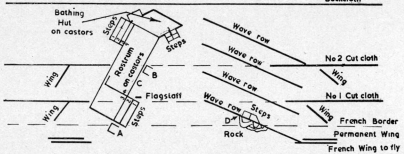

FIG. 32. GROUND PLAN, ACT II, SCENE 1.
LA PLAGE, EAUVILLE

A. Chair.   C. Railing with Bathing Towels. D. Rock, and
B. Chair.   Seaweed forming Trick cover for property
                   lobster used for business in this scene.
(By courtesy of Samuel French, Ltd.)

Denis de Marney

FIG. 33. ACT II, SCENE 1. LA PLAGE, EAUVILLE
(By courtesy of Samuel French, Ltd.)

Running Tabs ——————————————— Street Frontcloth ————————————

False Pros.

FIG. 34. ACT II, SCENE 2. A STREET, EAUVILLE. (FRONTCLOTH)
(By courtesy of Samuel French, Ltd.)

Denis de Marney

FIG. 35. ACT II, SCENE 2. A STREET, EAUVILLE
(By courtesy of Samuel French, Ltd.)

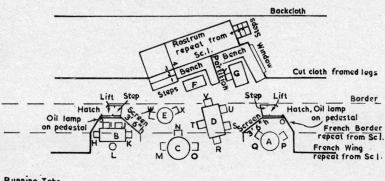

FIG. 36. GROUND PLAN, ACT II, SCENE 3.
CAFÉ DES POMMES, EAUVILLE

A to *G*. Tables. *H* to *K*, *M* to *Y*. Rush-seated chairs. *L*. Low wooden stool.
(By courtesy of Samuel French, Ltd.)

Denis de Marney

FIG. 37. ACT II, SCENE 3. THE CAFÉ DES POMMES, EAUVILLE
(By courtesy of Samuel French, Ltd.)

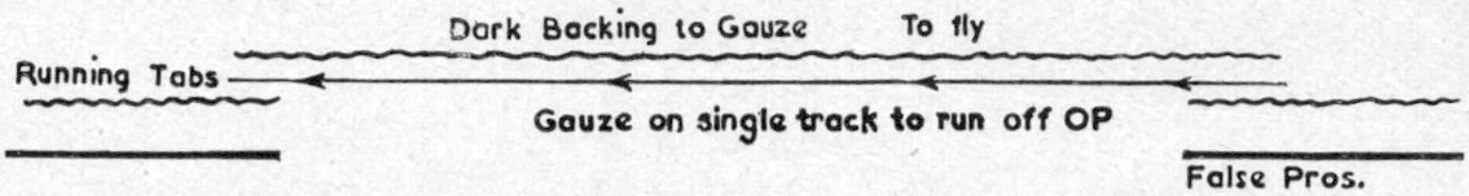

Dark Backing to Gauze   To fly

Running Tabs

Gauze on single track to run off OP

False Pros.

FIG. 38. ACT II, SCENE 4. PAINTED GAUZE FOR SLOW
FADE-IN TO ACT II, SCENE 5
(By courtesy of Samuel French, Ltd.)

Denis de Marney

FIG. 39. ACT II, SCENE 4. PAINTED GAUZE FOR SLOW
FADE-IN TO ACT II, SCENE 5
(By courtesy of Samuel French, Ltd.)

Act II, Scene 5 is the same as Act I, Scene 3

CHAPTER FOURTEEN

STAGE LIGHTING EQUIPMENT

EFFECTIVE lighting plays an important part in the presentation of a musical play. Good lighting can give character and brilliance to a scene which without it would appear dull and colourless. In most modern theatres to-day stage lighting equipment has reached a high state of efficiency, and includes the following items—

A switchboard with controls and dimmers.
Footlights.
Battens.
A spot bar.
Stage floods.
Stage spots.
Front-of-the-house equipment, consisting of spots or limes with long throws operated from a projection box at the back of the circle or gallery, and a battery of spots situated in front of the circle or upper circle.
In addition, many theatres can also provide pageants, lengths, extra spots, and acting-area floods. If these are not available as part of the standard equipment, they can be hired.

(All the illustrations in this chapter are reproduced by courtesy of Strand Electric and Engineering Co., Ltd.)

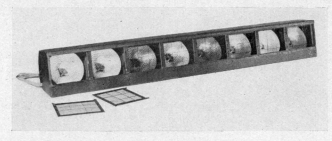

FIG. 40. FOOTLIGHTS
A six-foot section.

FIG. 41. A TWELVE-FOOT LIGHTING BATTEN SECTION

FIG. 42. A SLIDER DIMMER
One guard removed to show
internal detail.

FIG. 43. A PORTABLE SWITCHBOARD
Interlocking slider dimmer type (6-way).

Footlights and Battens

Footlights, or floats, throw light upwards from the stage level. Battens throw light downwards from above. Both consist of a series of lamps each housed in a separate box with a reflector. In front of each lamp is a frame which holds a colour

FIG. 44. A PERMANENT SWITCHBOARD
For schools and small halls, with 12 circuit dimmers fitted.

medium, or filter, which can be changed according to the colour required.

The lamps in the floats and battens are wired in three or four circuits. With four circuits for example, pink, amber, blue, and white can be used. Each circuit is on a separate dimmer which enables the intensity of each colour to be controlled from the switchboard.

Dimming circuits vary in different theatres. Some have

four circuits, some three, with resulting modifications of the colour changes available.

Spot Bar

This is a steel rod on which is fixed several spots. As described earlier, the spot bar is situated in front of No. 1 lighting

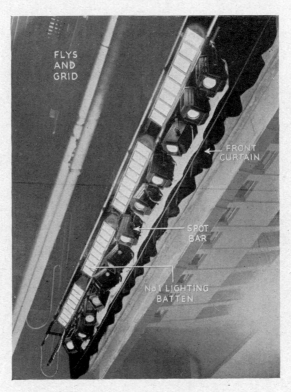

FIG. 45. SPOT BAR
Showing position in front of No. 1 Lighting Batten.

batten. The power of the lamps used on the spot bar varies; it is usually 500 or 1000 watts.

The value of a spot bar lies in the fact that powerful lights can be fixed and concentrated on any required parts of the acting area where important action takes place. Once the angles of the various lamps have been fixed they cannot be altered during the performance. With a fully-equipped spot bar with ten or more 1000 watt lamps, battens can often be dispensed with in certain scenes which lend themselves to special effects. In some cases, a full spot bar may carry a number of floods in addition to spots.

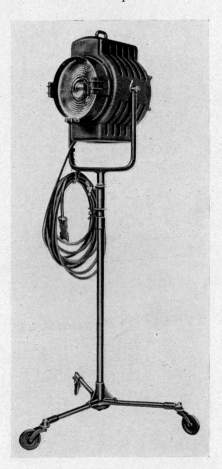

FIG. 46. 1000–2000-WATT SPOTLIGHT

For stage use where an intense soft-edged beam is required.

Perches

These are spots, preferably of 1000 watts, set at the side of the stage on a platform or "perch" about eight feet high and operated through apertures in the tormentors. In contrast to the fixed lamps in the spot bar, the angle of the perch spots can be altered as required during the performance.

Spots

The lamp in any spot, or focus-lantern as it is sometimes called, can be moved backwards and forwards so that the

FIG. 47. 500-WATT BABY SPOTLIGHT
For general stage use. For small stages it can also be used with effect
for lighting the forestage from the front of the house.

beam passing through the lens can be increased or diminished as required.

Baby spots are smaller editions of the 1000-watt type. 500-watt baby spots mounted on stands are usually operated from the wings. 250-watt and 100-watt baby spots are used for special effects in the scene itself. Concealed from the view of the audience behind furniture or a piece of scenery, they can be effectively used to concentrate localized light on a particular character or object, e.g. in a darkened room or in a night scene.

Baby spots, without stands, can also be set in the floats to

throw directional beams from a fixed position when required
during the performance.

FIG. 48. 100- OR 250-WATT FLOAT SPOTLIGHT
A small compact spotlight which can be concealed in footlights, stage
furniture, property fires, etc.

FIG. 49. BUILT-IN TYPE CIRCLE FRONT SPOTLIGHT HOUSING

Front-of-the-House Spots

Front-of-the-house spots are usually grouped as a battery
of six or more mirror spots in front of one of the circles. They

can be focused to a fine point like ordinary spots or set to flood the stage with a powerful and controllable beam of light which can be concentrated on any part of the acting area.

FIG. 50. 1000-WATT FRONT-OF-HOUSE MIRROR SPOTLIGHT
With a precision optical system which gives greater control of beam shape and spread than standard spotlights and more than three times the light output for the same wattage, according to beam spread.

For long throws, one or two powerful focus lanterns or limes from the back of the circle or gallery are used for pin-point spot lighting.

Floods

Unlike spots, floods have no lenses, and the light they give covers a much wider area. Wide-angle floods consist simply of a powerful lamp—usually 1000 watts—set in a housing with a reflector. The front of the flood is fitted with a colour frame.

A narrow-angle flood gives a more concentrated light on a more limited area.

Acting-area Floods or Arena Floods

These are floods in a special housing designed to cast a concentrated vertical beam of light on the stage from above. The

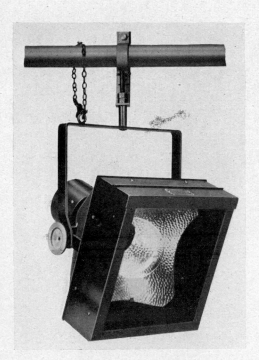

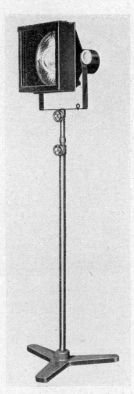

FIG. 51. 500-WATT BATTEN FLOOD

FIG. 52. 500-WATT WING FLOOD

For close range work such as lighting small backcloths and cycloramas.

lighting area thus projected from each lamp varies with its height above the stage, which of course can be adjusted as required. Acting area floods are fitted to take colour filters and diffusing screens.

Pageants

Pageants are specially designed floods which project a narrow concentrated shaft of light, e.g. to produce the effect of sunlight or moonlight through a window.

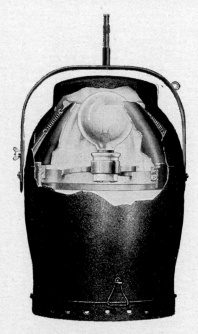

FIG. 53. 1000-WATT ACTING
AREA FLOOD
Giving a controlled but adjustable narrow-angle vertical beam.

FIG. 54. 1000-WATT PAGEANT LANTERN
Produces a very intense soft-edged narrow beam of light. Particularly suitable for simulating sunlight.

Groundrows

These are floats generally used for lighting backcloths and backings from the stage level. To be effective they have to be set far enough away from the object they are lighting. They are often placed behind a scenic groundrow or cut-out to illuminate the lower part of a backcloth.

Lengths and Strips

A length is a portable batten fitted with a number of electric bulbs. Lengths are usually hung on a hook at the back of a flat for lighting interior backings. Lengths used vertically behind scenic groundrows for lighting backcloths are also known as "strips."

Dips

Dips are traps let into the stage for plugging in floods, spots, and other lighting. They have a metal or wooden lid for protection when not in use. There are, as a rule, three or four dips on each side of the stage. By localizing the points in this way, long leads to the switchboard are avoided.

Tower

A tower is an upright batten of lights mounted on a base with wheels so that it can be quickly and easily moved into any desired position.

Boom

A stand designed to carry a vertical battery of floods for lighting backcloths from the sides of the stage.

Colour Mediums

These are the gelatine sheets used in lighting units to produce various colour effects. The wide range manufactured by Strand Electric and Engineering Co., Ltd., is in extensive use and a list of the colours available will be valuable for reference. The mediums are identified by their numbers, and guide samples are obtainable from the makers at 29 King Street, Covent Garden, London, W.C.2.

FIG. 55. MAGAZINE LENGTH FOR HANGING VERTICALLY OR HORIZONTALLY

For lighting window and door backings.

1. Yellow	8. Deep Salmon
2. Light Amber	9. Light Salmon
3. Straw	10. Middle Rose
4. Medium Amber	11. Dark Pink
5. Orange	12. Deep Rose
5A. Deep Orange	13. Magenta
6. Primary Red	14. Ruby
7. Light Rose	15. Peacock Blue

16. Blue Green
17. Steel Blue
18. Light Blue
19. Dark Blue
20. Deep Blue (Primary)
21. Pea Green
22. Moss Green
23. Light Green
24. Dark Green
25. Purple
26. Mauve
29. Heavy Frost
30. Clear
31. Light Frost
32. Medium Blue

33. Deep Amber
36. Pale Lavender (Surprise Pink)
38. Pale Green
39. Primary Green
40. Pale Blue
41. Bright Blue
42. Pale Violet
48. Bright Rose
49. Canary
50. Pale Yellow
51. Gold Tint
52. Pale Gold
53. Pale Salmon
54. Pale Rose

The following colours may be obtained by superimposing filters as follows—

Chocolate Tint. Superimpose 17, 50, 51
Pale Chocolate. Superimpose 17, 50, 53
Pale Grey.   Superimpose 17, 52, 17

A certain amount of caution is necessary when using colour mediums. Deep shades tend to alter colour values in scenery and costumes, and react unfavourably on make-up.

Pale Gold and Straw are useful for sunlight effects and do not seriously affect existing colour values; nor, to any appreciable extent, do Pale Lavender, Steel Blue, Pink, Pale Salmon, and Pale Rose. All are excellent for general lighting purposes.

The deeper shades such as Deep Amber, Magenta, Deep Orange, etc., are useful for effect lighting on backings and for other special purposes.

The various colour effects required throughout the show should be studied in detail to ensure that the fullest use is made of all fixed lighting available—the spot bar, acting-area and front-of-the-house lighting—which once set, cannot be altered. It is a good idea to mark on the ground plan for each scene the positions of principals, chorus, and dancing groups for the ensembles, finales, and other scenes with special lighting effects. The colour mediums for the fixed lighting and the remaining mediums for supplementary lighting (floats, battens, floods, pageants, and other spots) should be ordered well in advance of the lighting rehearsal, so that the producer can be sure of having the necessary material with which to obtain the results he has worked out from the lighting plot.

Producers will find much valuable information on lighting and other aspects of production in *"Tabs,"* a periodical published in the interests of the amateur theatre by Strand Electric and Engineering Co., Ltd. *"Tabs"* is obtainable without charge from the publishers at 29 King Street, Covent Garden, London, W.C.2.

STAGE DIMENSIONS AND EQUIPMENT

In considering spectacular musical shows for amateur production, it should be remembered that many were originally presented under exceptional conditions on large stages, with elaborate mechanical and lighting equipment not available in smaller theatres and halls.

Before deciding upon ambitious productions of this nature, those responsible in the society should satisfy themselves that the stage they propose to use is at least of adequate size, and possesses facilities for a reasonable reproduction of the original, although on a smaller scale.

As a matter of interest, the following stage dimensions and equipment of the Theatre Royal, Drury Lane, where *The Desert Song*, *Rose Marie*, *Glamorous Night*, *Oklahoma*, *Carousel*, *South Pacific*, and many other musical shows were first produced in Great Britain, give an indication of the extensive facilities in this famous theatre for spectacular presentation—

Proscenium width . . . . . 42 ft 6 in.
Proscenium height . . . . . 31 ft 6 in.
Stage depth from setting line . . . 78 ft 6 in.
Height of stage under fly galleries . . 26 ft 6 in.
Width of stage between fly galleries . . 60 ft
Height of grid from stage . . . . 72 ft
104 lines.
6 lifts.
Switchboard Electric Console—216 ways, each controlled by dimmer.
8 battens, four colours.
Footlights, four colours.
9 dips at each side of stage, four colours.
10 upper circle front-of-house spots, 1000 watts, four colours.
16 dress circle front-of-house spots, 1000 watts, four colours.
4 perches, 1000 watts.
3 front-of-house spots, 100 amp.
2 front-of-house floods, 60 amp.

Many large-scale musical shows have been successfully

produced by amateur societies at the Scala Theatre, London, where the main facilities include—

Proscenium width . . . . . 30 ft 6 in.
Proscenium height . . . . . 20 ft
Stage depth from setting line . . . 40 ft
Height under fly galleries . . . . 21 ft 10 in.
Width between fly galleries . . . 39 ft 6 in.
Height of grid from stage . . . . 63 ft
50 sets of lines.
Footlights, three circuits with independent dimmers.
5 battens, each with three circuits, independent dimmers.
Spot bar with 12 spots, each with independent dimmer control.
4 spots on stands.
4 floods on stands.
12 front-of-house pre-set spots with independent dimmers.

While excellent shows have been produced on smaller stages, the following is a good working average for general purposes—

Proscenium width . . . 28 ft.
Proscenium height . . . 20 ft.
Stage depth from setting line . . 30 ft.
Height under fly galleries . . 20 ft.
Width between fly galleries . . 32 ft.
Height of grid . . . . 40 ft.

These dimensions will permit of adequate presentation without undue modification of the standard scenery available on hire for most productions.

In halls where flying facilities are not available, the problems of quick scene changes can be overcome by the use of suitably designed running tabs, and by the adaptation of the script to allow for song reprises or action in front of the closed tabs while the next scene is being set up behind. If this is done, the requisite number of tab rails, as well as the tabs, should be hired if not included in the existing stage equipment.

CHAPTER FIFTEEN

MAKING THE MOST OF A SMALL STAGE

MANY societies find their choice of musical plays restricted because of limited stage facilities. Too often the only available hall possesses a very small stage with indifferent lighting and no space or equipment for flying scenery. It is surprising what can be done, however, if the production is specially designed to overcome the conditions imposed.

Scenery designed for a large stage and "made down" to fit a small stage is rarely satisfactory. The large-scale design of the sets looks out of place in the cramped space. The picture does not fit the frame. The stage becomes cluttered up with out-size wings, backings, borders, and so on, for which there is insufficient room, and the problems of scene-changing become almost insurmountable.

The secret of using a small stage to the best advantage is to suggest spaciousness by simple but effective scenic design. The designs of Stanley Haigh for *Cinderella* are an excellent example of how this result can be successfully achieved with the minimum amount of material.

A PRACTICAL EXAMPLE

The complete production was specially designed and built by Scenic Display Services of Bradford for use on stages without flying facilities and of approximately the following dimensions—

Proscenium width	.	. 25 ft
Depth to back wall	.	. 20 ft
Proscenium height	.	. 18 ft

A reasonable amount of side room is assumed, also facilities for hanging cloths and borders from girders or other fitments in the roof. Otherwise no special stage equipment is required.

The particular version of *Cinderella* for which this scenery was designed calls for nine scenes as follows—

ACT I

Scene	1.	A Woodland Glade	.	.	.	.	(Full Set)
,,	2.	The Ugly Sisters' Boudoir		.	.	.	(Frontcloth)
,,	3.	The Baron's Kitchen	.	.	.	.	(Half Set)
,,	4.	Transformation Scene from Kitchen to					
		Fairyland .	.	.	.	.	(Full Set)

ACT II

Scene	1.	The Palace Ballroom	.	.	.	.	(Full Set)
,,	2.	The Way Home	.	.	.	.	(Frontcloth)
,,	3.	The Baron's Conservatory		.	.	.	(Full Set)
,,	4.	The Forest .	.	.	.	.	(Frontcloth)
,,	5.	The Palace: Cinderella's Wedding .		.	.	(Full Set)

As each Act must run straight through without a break, the problems of scene changing, involving five full sets, appear formidable without flying facilities. By skilful design and construction, however, a smooth-running production is made possible on a small stage.

BASIC CONSTRUCTION

Starting with the empty stage, a sky cloth is hung on three lines from the roof as near the back wall as possible, leaving sufficient room for the cast to cross the stage behind the cloth for their entrances on either side.

The sky cloth serves as a cyclorama backing for scenic ground rows or cut-outs, and a small space is allowed for these between the cloth and a rostrum, constructed in four sections, each 6 ft long, 3 ft wide, and 18 in. high. Ramps are added to each end for entrances and for moving Cinderella's coach on and off the rostrum for the Finale of Act 1.

Next, a permanent architectural structure of flats, bolted together to form a complete French flat, is hung from the roof on three lines so that it stands upright in front of the rostrum.

Two neutral grey festoon borders and four drape wings or "legs" to match, two on each side of the stage, are hung on battens. The wings are fixed in position on the stage by battens at the foot.

Two 6-in. steps are placed in front of the 18-in. rostrum at the three archways, thus providing three steps in all, each 6 in. high.

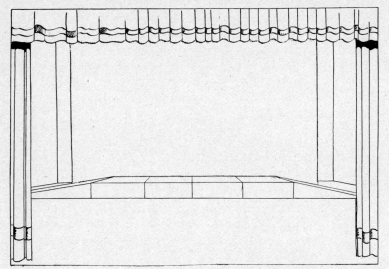

FIG. 56. THE ROSTRUM AND SKY CLOTH IN POSITION

FIG. 57. THE BASIC CONSTRUCTION

In order to effect the various changes, five sets of tab rails are required to operate five running tabs, the purpose of which will be explained later. These are additional to the house tabs.

There is also a special floral border for Act I, Scene 4, which is folded out of sight during the other scenes and lowered when required. This border is "cleared" during the interval.

This completes the basic structure from which the scenes are derived.

THE SCENES IN DETAIL

Act I, Scene 1: A Woodland Glade

The first scene is now built up as follows—

Four tree flats are secured with tape tied round the four basic uprights in front of the rostrum. These are "cut-outs" with wide foliage tops which overlap each other slightly at the top of the arches when placed in position. The structure to which they are fixed is now completely covered. The two tree flats *L.* and *R.* of the rostrum are wider than those in the centre, and are hinged to provide returns for masking entrances up-stage.

Four 4-ft hinged wings, two at each side, are now added.

For this scene two woodland foliage borders are hung on battens in front of the festoon borders. At the end of the scene, if space in the roof permits, the woodland borders are raised clear of the festoon borders which serve for all remaining full sets. If there is not sufficient clearance in the roof to do this the foliage borders can be hung *behind* the festoon borders. The draped loops of the festoon borders are thrown back out of sight over the battens so that the woodland borders are left clear. At the end of the scene the festoon borders are pushed over their battens with a long pole so that they fall into position in front of the woodland borders to cover them completely.

A landscape groundrow is set in front of the sky cloth, and imitation grass carpeting fitted round the foot of the trees and over the steps, to give the effect of a grassy slope. A tree log *R.,* also dressed with imitation grass, completes the scene.

Act I, Scene 2: The Boudoir

The house tabs close on Scene 1. Decorative tabs with a fleur-de-lys motif are brought in on tab rail No. 3, just behind

Fig. 58. Act I, Scene 1. A Woodland Glade

Fig. 59. Act I, Scene 2. The Boudoir

No. 1 festoon border and the two down-stage drape wings, now revealed by the removal of the tree wings. A gold dressing table, stool, and chaise longue are placed in position *C*. This is a simple, quick change.

Act I, Scene 3: The Baron's Kitchen

While Scene 2 is being played, Scene 3 is being set. The cloth for this is painted on a gauze operated on tab rail No. 4.

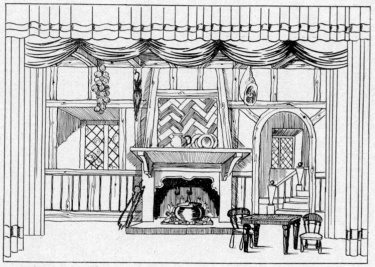

Fig. 60. Act I, Scene 3. The Baron's Kitchen

Immediately behind, on tab rail No. 5, are black velvet tabs which are closed behind the gauze immediately in front of the rostrum.

The tree wings from Scene 1 have been removed to reveal the drape wings of the basic setting. The other changes which have been made behind the black velvet tabs relate to the transformation scene, and will be described later.

In front of the gauze backcloth for the kitchen scene a fireplace set, complete with glowing log fire, cauldron and other properties, occupies the centre of the stage. This fireplace set is constructed in two halves mounted on trucks. When the trucks are wheeled away in opposite directions, the fireplace divides to reveal the scene behind it.

This is the scene in which the Fairy Godmother grants Cinderella's wish and provides the golden coach to take her to the Ball.

As the Fairy casts her spell there is a stage blackout on a given cue, leaving the stage in darkness except for the glow of the fire. While she performs the magic rites over the cauldron, punctuated by electrically-operated flashes, the black velvet tabs are slowly opened behind the gauze. Blue flood lighting is gradually brought up to full on the rostrum. A fairy ballet is seen through the gauze.

On the last flash which accompanies the magic spell, the gauze tabs are slowly opened. Simultaneously, the fireplace divides and the two halves are wheeled off to each side of the stage. The stage hands who do this operate behind the truck and are, of course, unseen by the audience. When the fireplace divides, Cinderella is discovered seated in the illuminated golden coach on the rostrum.

Within a minute the scene has changed from kitchen to Fairyland. The rostrum is framed with flowers. By the use of changing colours in the lighting this transformation scene, which includes a fairy ballet, is highly effective.

The transformation setting is achieved very simply as follows—

When the kitchen scene is being set, and while it is being played, the woodland tree flats are untied, removed from the permanent architectural structure, and replaced with floral uprights which are tied in position round the basic columns.

The woodland groundrow and rostrum steps are taken away. A floral groundrow is placed in position against the flat face of the rostrum. Above, a deep floral border, referred to earlier, has been hung from the roof and "tumbled," i.e. folded and secured with clips so that it is out of sight until required. The clips are released and the border is dropped down into position.

There is no groundrow against the sky cloth in this scene, which depends to a great extent for its effect upon the illuminated coach, and lighting.

During the blackout prior to the transformation, floral wings are slid in unobstrusively to cover the drape wings.

With so many things happening at once, this scene change

FIG. 61. ACT I, SCENE 4. THE TRANSFORMATION;
THE FIREPLACE DIVIDES

FIG. 62. ACT I, SCENE 4. THE FINAL SCENE AFTER
THE TRANSFORMATION

calls for a reliable and well-rehearsed stage staff, and although such a complicated production routine is unusual in the average musical play, it shows what can be done with limited resources.

Act II, Scene 1 : The Palace Ballroom

Act II opens with a beautiful ballroom scene in white and gold. Flats are secured to the basic structure as in previous

FIG. 63. ACT II, SCENE 1. THE PALACE BALLROOM

scenes, and in this case the centre steps only are used for the rostrum.

The groundrow in front of the sky cloth is an elaborate cut-out with a large clock as the centre piece. The hands of the clock are moved round gradually as the scene proceeds, by means of a thread mechanism, until they point to midnight for Cinderella's departure from the Ball. The furniture—chairs and ornamental tables—is in crimson and gold.

Act II, Scene 2 : The Way Home

Decorative tabs, as illustrated on p. 176, are used on the tab rail No. 1 for this scene.

FIG. 64. ACT II, SCENE 2. THE WAY HOME

FIG. 65. ACT II, SCENE 3. THE BARON'S CONSERVATORY

Act II, Scene 3 : The Baron's Conservatory

The conservatory scene is set while the previous scene is being played. The Palace flats are untied and replaced by four trellis flats. The clock is removed and a garden groundrow placed in front of the sky cloth. Two sets of rostrum steps are added, and tables and chairs placed in position.

FIG. 66. ACT II, SCENE 4. THE FOREST

Act II, Scene 4 : The Forest

Decorative tabs, suggesting a woodland scene, are operated here on tab rail No. 2.

Act II, Scene 5 : The Palace: Cinderella's Wedding

For the final scene the conservatory flats are removed while the previous scene is being played. The basic structure itself is used for this Palace set with the addition of electric lights on the flats. This is simply and quickly done and only involves fixing the candle-lamp brackets and plugging in. Centre steps only are used, and a Palace groundrow completes the scene.

This scenic plan for a small stage can be applied with equal effect to many musical shows with several scenes. Societies who hesitate to stage such productions under restricted conditions with ordinary hired scenery may find a little bold experiment on these lines well worth while. It will be appreciated that much depends upon simple and effective design, and an art director with the necessary artistic ability and stage sense can be most useful in this connexion. Most contractors are generally willing

FIG. 67. ACT II, SCENE 5. FINALE. THE PALACE

to make up special scenery from stock material, based on sketches submitted by the society.

MAKING OR HIRING?

Is it worth while for an operatic society to make its own scenery? The answer depends largely upon the workshop and storage facilities available. The leading hiring contractors to-day can supply complete sets of scenery for most of the popular musical shows in sizes to fit most stages. To make its own scenery on this scale, a society would have to set up a studio and workshop large enough for design, construction, and storage of timber, canvas, rostrums, flats, backcloths, and all the material and equipment required for the job. The construction and painting of scenery needs a lot of space, and the cost of suitable premises, especially in towns, plus the materials, would far exceed the hiring charges for the average musical production.

In the case of straight plays, it is a fairly simple matter to adapt the scenery of one production, e.g. a room interior, to suit another. The basic construction of flats, doors, windows, fireplaces, etc., can always be modified where necessary, re-painted, and rearranged at little expense. With musical plays, however, the scenery is more elaborate and the locale so entirely different in each case that, with few exceptions, it is usually cheaper to hire.

Smaller societies who can find workshop premises at low cost—a barn, school accommodation, or a garage, for example —may find it profitable to make their own scenery for small stages, provided it is designed on the simple stylized lines described earlier in this chapter. Given the enthusiasm, the aptitude, and the facilities, it is possible to make very effective scenery on these lines within a reasonable budget.

DESIGN AND CONSTRUCTION

Design is all-important, and the services of someone with a flair for this type of creative work should be enlisted as art director. Through clever design it is possible to make a small stage look larger than it is. The secret lies in a simplicity and economy of design which can suggest depth and space by the use of rostrums and simple groundrows, in conjunction with a skycloth or cyclorama.

Flats of various kinds will be required. These can be con-structed of 3 in. by 1 in. seasoned timber in 3-ft, 4-ft, or 6-ft widths to any required height.

The corners of the frame should be mortised and tenoned, with two horizontal rails mortised into shoes (or toggles) to give additional rigidity. In the larger sizes two corner cross braces should be added for extra strength. (See illustration on page 141.)

Good quality flax canvas should be used and tightly stretched over the frame. To do this the canvas can be secured tem-porarily by fixing it at each corner with a tack, and then stretching the canvas progressively all round as it is finally tacked home. The edge of the canvas should be folded in and glued before the tacks are driven home. Flats are supported by braces, and secured in position by lines and cleats as described on pages 141-2.

Fitting doors, windows, and archways into the flats presents no great constructional difficulty, apart from ensuring that the additional framework to which they are fitted is sufficiently strong and rigid.

For profile edges and groundrow cut-outs, three-ply wood or profile board should be used.

In making backcloths, it will be necessary to join the strips of canvas to obtain the required height. The canvas should be joined horizontally, never vertically. When joined, it should be battened at the top, stretched, and then battened at the bottom.

PAINTING

To paint scenery the canvas must be primed first with a mixture of size and whiting in the proportions of 1 lb of size to a gallon of primer. Hot water should be used for making the size solution, which is added to sufficient whiting to give a creamy consistency when thoroughly stirred. The primer should be applied when warm. When the primer is thoroughly dry, painting can begin. Colours are obtainable in powder form and mixed with a solution of size to the desired shade.

Sketches of the scenes should be made first, and then working drawings or models prepared to scale.

The design and construction of scenery present many technical problems. Broad simple effects both in colour and design should be aimed at. What may appear crude and garish at close quarters will look entirely different with full stage lighting from the auditorium.

A certain amount of technical information can be gleaned from textbooks, but much depends on the artistic ability and stage sense of the designer, and whether he can create practical designs which will look effective *on the lighted stage*. This is a matter of experiment with drawing and model.

The society's carpenter should be able to deal with the building and construction, otherwise it is advisable to employ a professional craftsman for this work.

SHELL SETTING.
ILLUMINATED PYLONS. ROSTRUMS & STEPS.
SHELLS IN RELIEF.

SCENIC
DISPLAY
SERVICES
BRADFORD

FIG. 68. ROUGH SKETCH FOR A SIMPLE BUT EFFECTIVE FULL-STAGE
SET, USING DRAPERIES, ROSTRUMS, AND SHELL CUT-OUT

FIG. 69. ROUGH SKETCH FOR A BACKCLOTH

THE ART OF IMPROVISATION

Many operatic works have been successfully produced on a small stage by skilful improvisation. If those responsible for the production fully understand the purpose and use of modern stage equipment, the task of scaling things down, of adapting existing facilities, and adding to them to the best advantage, becomes a comparatively simple matter.

We have seen in earlier chapters how a large theatre stage is constructed and equipped, and how the various types of scenery and lighting apparatus are used to produce varying effects. All the features of the big stage can be reproduced effectively, with a reasonable amount of skill and imagination, on a small stage. We have seen, too, how scenery can be simplified in design to suggest space; how it can be constructed to provide for swift and easy changes where "flying" facilities do not exist.

If the society or school group is in the happy position of being able to hire lighting equipment to make good deficiencies, improvisation is an easy matter. If, on the other hand, insufficient funds will not permit of hiring, much of this equipment can be made with simple materials at little cost.

Lighting on the stage is derived, as we have already seen, from six main sources—light from battens above, light from footlights in front of the stage at ground-level, lights from spot bar and acting-area lamps, and light from floods and spots on the stage and from the front of the house.

Before proceeding to make up improvised lighting equipment, however, it should be ascertained from a reliable source whether the existing installation is capable of carrying the increased electrical load. The local electricity authority or electrician should be consulted on this and other points, to make sure that whatever is done is both safe and sound. The local electrician will, as a rule, be glad to offer advice on technical matters, and suggest the best and cheapest methods of wiring as well as the most effective types of lamps to use.

Battens can be rigged up with horizontal strips of wood, the lamp bulbs being set in metal boxes with reflectors. The boxes should be provided with adequate ventilation holes, and with clips on the front to carry colour mediums. Dimmers are, of course, most effective; if funds permit, they can be hired through the local electrician.

It is not beyond the capacity of the enterprising handyman to construct a simple "tower" of two or three floods housed in large metal boxes with reflectors, and mounted on a vertical batten on a stand. Reflectors can be made either with sheet tin or aluminium. Three clips should be fitted on the front of the improvised housing to slide in and secure colour mediums. These towers are ideal for backcloth lighting, and should be used in conjunction with a groundrow for bottom lighting and a batten for lighting the cloth from above.

Effective area lighting can be obtained by using large deep industrial metal shades adapted to take colour mediums.

If it is possible to hire a spot bar, footlights can often be dispensed with. Footlights, however, can be made up in much the same way as the battens, and should, if possible, be sunk into the stage so that the housing is not visible to the audience.

It will be necessary to hire front-of-the-house spots and limes if these are considered necessary, unless existing slide lanterns or film projectors can be brought into service.

It should be remembered that too much lighting should be avoided on a small stage. It is neither necessary nor advisable to flood everything with intense light. It is contrast and balance that matter in relation to the size of the stage and the auditorium. The lighting for a musical show must, of course, be adequate and it must have *depth*. The backing or skycloth should be brightly and evenly lit, but not with glaring white light. Colour mediums should be used according to the effect required—pink or amber are useful colours—and the rest of the stage lighting from battens, footlights, and other sources should be suitably distributed to render the scene, however simple it may be, as colourful and interesting as possible.

The front curtain often presents difficulty on a small stage. Curtain and tab rails can be hired, or they can be purchased and fitted permanently if the same hall is used regularly for operatic performances. The curtains and runners should be thoroughly tested before each performance. The timing of a "curtain" is most important, whether the tabs are flown or drawn at the end of an act or scene. Curtains which stick or will not close smoothly may ruin the dramatic effect of a scene. Even if tab rails with proper runners are beyond the means of a young struggling society, curtains hung by rings on an ordinary rod or strong wire can be made to operate smoothly if fitted with cords for opening and closing.

Even where scenery has been successfully designed to suggest space on a small stage, and lighting problems have been overcome, the whole effect can be neutralized by having too many people on the stage. A small but efficient chorus which can be properly grouped to form a pleasing picture, is to be preferred to a large chorus which fills every square inch of the stage, so that the audience cannot see the scene. Rostrums help to overcome this difficulty; they also add interest to the design and are especially useful when there is no rake on the stage. The chorus can be more effectively grouped at different levels, and the appearance of overcrowding eliminated to some extent.

A model stage is a valuable aid to effective improvisation. Aspiring young producers will find this a fascinating and practical means of mastering many of the problems of stagecraft. Scenic design and even lighting can be experimented with, and ideas worked out before putting them into practice. With a model stage, the intelligent use of sets made to scale quickly develops a sense of composition, and for working out production details it is invaluable.

CHAPTER SIXTEEN

OTHER PRODUCTION MATTERS

HAVING discussed music, scenery, and lighting, we can now turn our attention to some other matters which must be considered before it is possible to present a show.

COSTUMES

As with scenery, hiring usually works out more cheaply than making, especially when there are several changes of costume. With a comparatively simple production, however, it might be worth while on occasion for a society to make its own costumes.

An art director can be most useful, not only in the matter of design and historical accuracy if the society has chosen a period show, but in suggesting cheap, colourful material which will look effective on the stage. A clever art director can often work wonders if he has full control over the design of scenery, costumes, and furnishings. By employing a bold, simple technique he can often create a production of beauty and distinction at moderate cost.

Stage costumes are designed for effect. What they look like on the stage, under varying stage lighting, and in the setting, is the most important consideration. The material with which they are made, the style, and the finish must not be compared with ordinary standards of dressmaking. Stage costumes must be very smartly cut. They must fit well. In style they can be exaggerated to emphasize line and colour. What looks rich and stylish on the stage may be made with the cheapest of material which would not bear close examination in ordinary light.

It is possible to obtain good results by painting material with gold, silver, and colour. Flowers, transfers, and gaily-coloured designs can be used on plain material to produce exciting effects in colour. Materials can also be effectively dyed in special shades to suit various groupings.

The costumes should be considered in relation to the scene, and in his work of design the art director should produce complete colour roughs or even models showing the costumes in their correct groupings in the various scenes. From these roughs, large-scale drawings in colour should be prepared to bring out detail. There are several excellent books on stage costume, and a wealth of reference material in the form of prints and pictures in the libraries and art galleries.

If a society does decide to make its own costumes for a production, this must be done thoroughly and with a full appreciation of the enormous labour involved. Badly-designed work is worse than useless. If the whole job cannot be carried through with the necessary enthusiasm and help from many willing hands, it should not be embarked upon.

The society's wardrobe managers should be given charge of the actual making of the costumes, and a team of volunteers organized to carry out the work. In musical shows with modern dress it is often worth while for a society to make its own ladies' costumes, although an arrangement can probably be made with a local firm to supply a range of suitable dresses at a special rate, in return for an acknowledgment and advertising space in the programme.

When hiring costumes, the wardrobe master and wardrobe mistress are responsible for taking the correct measurements, and entering all details on the form provided for the purpose by the contractor. If at all possible, a representative of the society should pay a visit to the contractor's premises and discuss the costume requirements on the spot. If an appointment is arranged in advance, the representative—the art director, the wardrobe mistress, or other official—will not only be able to discuss terms and other details, but will also have an opportunity of seeing the actual range of costumes available. It may be possible to cover the costume plot by using more effective costumes from other productions in place of the usual stock supply for the show concerned. This makes a personal call well worth while if the society's funds will permit.

FURNITURE

Furniture for a musical show should be kept down to the absolute minimum, both in quantity and size. For historical shows the period should be carefully studied, and reproduction furniture selected as near the date as possible. Sometimes secondhand furniture can be picked up cheaply at shops and auction sales. It may look very dilapidated, but provided the style is correct and the construction sound, it can be very easily restored and renovated by an efficient stage carpenter. Gold paint and new silk coverings can completely transform old furniture for the stage.

Apart from pieces definitely called for in the action, furniture used to decorate the set and suggest the atmosphere of the play should be kept down to the minimum. It should, however, be chosen with care, and the art director can very often make useful suggestions for its most effective use. A few good, well-arranged pieces which blend unobtrusively into the scene are to be preferred to large ostentatious furniture which fills the stage and gets in everybody's way.

Large stage carpets are expensive to hire. A stage cloth, painted a plain colour, or with an appropriate carpet design, makes an effective substitute.

PROPERTIES

The property list for a musical show can involve considerable expense if every item is hired. The list should be gone through to determine whether many of the articles could not be more cheaply purchased or made by members of the society.

Many simple hand props can, of course, be provided by the artistes concerned—cigarette cases, lighters, wallets, fountain-pens, and so on. Effective stage jewellery can be made up from cheap trinkets. Milliner's hat-boxes can be converted to the stage variety by covering them with wallpaper of appropriate design.

The property master can, with a little ingenuity and resource, find ways and means of acquiring, or making, most of the stage and hand properties required for the average musical show.

Some properties can often be obtained free from the makers in return for the usual acknowledgment in the programme. Telephones, for example, are frequently loaned by the G.P.O. on this basis. Proprietary items such as cigarettes, cosmetics, etc., for stage purposes, will be supplied by the manufacturers free in certain circumstances.

EFFECTS

Stage effects are of two kinds—visual and sound. Nowadays, most effects are produced on modern mechanical devices, although some are still obtained by simpler and more direct methods.

The effects lantern is one of the mechanical devices used for visual effects. It is used to project drifting clouds, snow, fireworks, and other effects on a backcloth.

The reproduction of sound effects on the stage has been revolutionized by the use of sound recordings. These sound discs are supplied by the leading gramophone companies, and cover a wide range. They can be obtained on order through most music dealers. The records must be played on a panatrope or radiogram of adequate volume. Most theatres are now equipped with panatropes. The instrument should be tested before each performance.

Effects should be thoroughly rehearsed. Also, a certain amount of experiment will be necessary before they are perfect. Badly-timed effects can often ruin a scene and it is worth while spending some time in getting them right.

Sounds such as ringing telephones, door bells, slamming doors, etc., should come from the right direction, e.g. when the front door is on stage L. the door bell should ring off L.

Sound effects obtainable from sound discs include: Aeroplane effects, car noises, train noises, sea and ship noises, wind, thunderstorm, war noises, and heavy gun-fire; animal noises, crowd noises, off-stage music, church bells, and organ music, etc.

Other effects can be very convincingly produced with simple apparatus, e.g.—

Thunder. This is produced by means of a thunder sheet—an iron sheet about 6 ft × 3 ft suspended by ropes. The effect is obtained by shaking the sheet.

Revolver shots. Hit a leather cushion smartly with a thin stick, or use a safety pistol which fires caps.

Loud explosion. An electrically-controlled charge detonated in a dust-bin.

Door slam. Slam a real door. There is usually one sufficiently near the stage. Failing this, a door slam can be used. This is a door, complete with lock and frame, set up for the purpose off-stage.

Telephone bells. Telephone bells and buzzers are operated by a press button from the prompt corner.

Door knocker. Fit a knocker to a solid piece of wood.

Horses hooves. Use two halves of a coco-nut shell. They should be "knocked" on a hard surface, e.g. on a wall for road or street effects, on a leather pad for turf.

Rain. Roll peas on a large drum. For visual rain drop rice from the flys through a trough. The falling rice must be properly lit to get the desired effect, and there must be an adequate supply to sustain it. Real water from sprays can also be used, but as this involves a trough and drain to take the water away, elaborate precautions are necessary and the simpler method is advised.

Wind. The sound of wind can be effectively produced from a wind machine, which is simply a slatted wooden drum fitted on a spindle with a handle attached. A piece of coarse canvas is stretched over the drum and secured to the base at each side of the drum. When the handle is turned the sound of wind is produced by the slats on the drum rubbing against the canvas shield.

CHAPTER SEVENTEEN

THE FINAL REHEARSALS

THE weeks of hard work should now be bearing fruit, and by the time the producer has progressed through the preparatory stages to the final rehearsals, he should be concentrating on giving the show pace, style, and polish.

By this time, too, the stage manager and his staff should be fully conversant with their duties, for production is not only painstaking rehearsal but also careful organization. Dialogue, action, and music should be merging into a composite whole, and what has been up to now an uneven patchwork should be taking on continuity and shape. It is at this point that an imaginative producer can, during the few remaining hours at his disposal, give the production the touch of spontaneity, sparkle, and *personality* which will raise it above the ordinary.

Living with a production through rehearsal after rehearsal tends to deaden the critical faculties. A feeling of staleness is liable to creep into the proceedings unless the producer can· keep the enthusiasm up to concert pitch right through to the end. There is nothing worse in this vital phase of production than over-confidence, a feeling that all that can be done has been done, and that everyone can relax until the opening performance.

PRODUCTION POINTS

During the final rehearsals the producer should pay special attention to the pace and *tempo* of the show. This does not mean that the players should merely speak and move faster, or that the chorus should race through their numbers. This is almost as bad as playing the show too slowly. There must be *tempo*, i.e. effective timing, as well as pace. It is the right combination of both which produces *rhythmic* speed. This can be achieved only if chorus and principals alike are alert and ready for their entrances and cues.

Dialogue, whether brisk and bright in comedy scenes, or

emotionally expressive in romantic scenes, should flow rhyth-
mically and naturally. Musical numbers should be put over
with vivacity and confidence. The singers should give the
impression that they hold the initiative. The dull, heavy effect
of some amateur solo work is due largely to lack of attack which
slows the singer down. It is the job of the producer, in consultation with the musical director, to correct this basic fault.
Musical comedy and light opera should be gay and spontaneous
—champagne, not flat beer.

Another production fault is an unduly long wait between
scenes. The producer should make provision for possible time
lags which might occur through lack of adequate stage facilities. A show with several scenes should flow smoothly without
hitches, and if there are likely to be any, something should be
planned ahead to fill them in should the necessity arise. The
introduction of a new short scene, some additional dialogue,
or a reprise of a previous number in front of running tabs, will
at least fill in the gap while the next scene is being set behind.
In the case of awkward changes on a limited stage, it is often
a good idea, if practicable, to end a scene by closing the tabs
behind the characters as they move down-stage, so that they
can go straight into their reprise or extra dialogue without any
interruption to the performance.

Over-repetition of the same piece of music from the orchestra
should be avoided between scenes when there is a long wait due
to some unforeseen hitch backstage. The producer should be
aware of the stage difficulties beforehand, and agree with the
musical director on the music to be played in such an emergency.

Encores should be kept down to a minimum. It is better to
leave the audience wanting more than to take advantage of
every tribute of applause. The routine of taking encores should
be carefully rehearsed so that the musical director and the
players know what to do. The professional technique is to
give the impression that the artistes concerned do not wish to
hold up the show, but that the applause is so overwhelming
that the producer or stage manager has waived the rules and
signalled to them to take the encore. Not entirely ethical,
perhaps, but nevertheless effective.

Crowd scenes and ensembles sometimes lack conviction

because of inadequate rehearsal. In these big scenes everyone
—principals and chorus—should be given something specific
to do, not only in action but in dialogue as well. A bright
animated market scene, for instance, will never be made bright
and animated merely by telling the company to move about
the stage and make a noise like a market. All should be
given parts in character with specially written lines. Arrange
groups, pair some off together, make others work singly, then
move them around so that they join others. Tell them where
to go and what to say. Design the movements to give the
impression of bustle and excitement: a policeman moving on
a couple of sparring toughs; a sailor talking to a girl; a beggar
asking for alms; a cheeky little boy reprimanded by his
parents for over-precocious behaviour; a street trader offering
his wares; and so on, according to the scene. All this kind of
purposeful movement woven into a carefully worked out
pattern, with a babel of actual rehearsed dialogue and laughter
going on simultaneously, will produce the desired result quickly
and effectively.

During the final rehearsals the producer may find it necessary
to tighten up discipline considerably. Not that discipline should
have been lacking in previous rehearsals, but up till now he will
have been getting his results in the preparatory stages by
patience and quiet persuasion. His time will have been occupied in showing the cast how they should act, move correctly,
give their lines full expression, and put their numbers over to
the best effect. At times it may seem that the chorus and
dancers have progressed far ahead of the principals. With only
a few more rehearsals, a new sense of urgency must be introduced into the proceedings, and the producer must voice his
opinion firmly if any members of the cast are not keeping pace
with general progress after all the hard instructional work
which has been expended on them.

THE DRESS PARADE

Societies which are fortunate enough to obtain facilities for
more than one dress rehearsal can combine their final run-
through of the show with a dress parade on the actual stage on
which the performances will take place. As a rule, however,
when the show is being presented for a week's run in a theatre,

it will not be possible to set up the scenery and hold the dress rehearsal until the Sunday before the first performance on the Monday night. In this case a dress parade should be arranged in the rehearsal rooms, or in other suitable premises, on the previous Friday or Saturday, or earlier, according to when the costumes are available.

The object of the dress parade is to enable the master and mistress of the robes to check all details of the costumes, so that necessary adjustments can be effected in time, and any omissions made good before the first night at the latest. The dress parade also gives the producer and dance producer an idea of how well the costumes are going to fit in with the groupings and routines they have worked out during rehearsals. It may be necessary, in order to keep the harmonies right and avoid harsh clashes of colour, to alter some of the groups slightly, and this may involve additional rehearsals.

The cast should be seen in their positions in costume for the opening choruses, main ensembles, and finales for each act. Similarly, all details of principals' costumes should be carefully checked. If it is convenient to have the final pre-dress rehearsal in costume on the same day as the dress parade, so much the better.

THE FINAL REHEARSAL

This is the last opportunity the producer will have of seeing the performance right through before the dress rehearsal. On this occasion he should let the rehearsal go through without stopping, and announce the fact to the company beforehand.

The stage manager will time the complete performance accurately, to confirm previous estimates and make sure that there is sufficient margin for all scene and costume changes.

The producer and dance producer should make their final critical assessment of the performance. If the cast know that there will be no hold-ups in this rehearsal they will be less "on edge" as the performance proceeds, thus giving the producer a more reliable idea how they are going to shape on the first night of the show. An uninterrupted rehearsal will also be of value to the musical director in checking over his cues and any last-minute alterations he may have made to the score and orchestrations. It is, of course, a great advantage if the orchestra can attend this final rehearsal in full strength as it will accustom the cast to the full orchestral accompaniment of their numbers.

The prompter should make a special note of any dialogue passages which may need attention at the dress rehearsal and on the opening night. Indeed, all production staff should now be fully prepared for all eventualities so that the dress rehearsal may proceed as smoothly as possible.

The question of inviting a small selected audience to the final rehearsal should be carefully weighed up. It depends a great deal upon whether such persons can visualize what the performance they see in the comparatively drab surroundings of the rehearsal room will be like in the more glamorous atmosphere of the theatre, with scenery, lighting, and effects. It is safer, perhaps, to exclude strangers on this occasion, as a wrong impression gained under unfavourable circumstances can soon circulate round the neighbourhood to the detriment of the show.

At the end of the rehearsal, the cast should be given a break while the producer compares notes with the dance producer, musical director, and stage manager. The cast should then be reassembled, and all rough sequences in the show rehearsed and polished up, until all points requiring attention have been disposed of to the satisfaction of the producer. If everyone has pulled his weight under an efficient producer, this recapitulation should not be a lengthy business and will serve to smooth out difficulties, and avoid hitches which might prolong the dress rehearsal unduly. It is better to get rid of the remaining rough spots in the show on the same day as the final rehearsal, when all the details are fresh in everyone's mind.

CHAPTER EIGHTEEN

THE DRESS REHEARSAL

THE old clichés "It'll be all right on the night" and "a bad dress rehearsal means a good show" should not be taken too seriously. They are generally expressions of hope rather than statements of fact. A bad dress rehearsal is more often a sign of inadequate preparation and lack of organization than an indication of better things to come.

THE PRELIMINARIES

If everything has been properly rehearsed and organized beforehand there is no reason why any dress rehearsal should go on for hours beyond the normal time. It should commence early enough to allow for a complete performance of the show, with some additional time after each scene to run through any items not up to the standard required by the producer.

If the society is fortunate enough to have access (some days before the opening performance) to the theatre or other building in which the show is being produced, the work of preparation can be more comfortably planned in advance. Assuming, however, that the dress rehearsal, and the preparations for it, must be conducted under the most exacting conditions, i.e. in a theatre on the Sunday prior to the opening on the Monday night, careful organization is necessary to ensure that everything will be ready in time.

Arrangements should be made for early morning delivery of the scenery, furniture, properties, costumes, extra lighting and other equipment. If possible, the scenery and costumes should be delivered first. The costumes will have to be unpacked and laid out by the wardrobe department for attention. The scenery will be checked on arrival against the scene plot so that the work of setting it up can begin as soon as possible. Furniture, properties, and equipment should all follow later so that their arrival does not interfere with the sorting out of the scenery.

The dress rehearsal call for the company should be made for at least one hour before the rise of the curtain. If it is a big production, with several scene changes, it is likely to be a trying day for the production staff, and an early morning start is desirable.

Before the dress rehearsal, the stage manager should have made the necessary arrangements for the delivery of all material to the theatre. In some cases it may be possible to effect delivery on the Saturday if there is sufficient space available backstage, and the current show moving out is not a heavy one.

The theatre electrician should also have been advised, some time in advance, of the electrical requirements and lighting plot so that he can make his arrangements accordingly. Theatre lighting equipment which may not have been in use for some time will have to be looked out and reconditioned, and the longest possible notice of this should be given.

Similarly, the scene plot will indicate the number of battens, tab rails, etc., necessary for the production, and it is the stage manager's responsibility to make sure in advance that when the scenery arrives, the apparatus for setting it up and operating it will be available.

The property master is responsible for checking in the furniture and properties against the property plot, and for arranging stand-by tables for the hand props at each side of the stage, so that they are conveniently available for the artistes near their entrances.

Similarly, the wardrobe department will check in the costumes and arrange them in the dressing-rooms ready for the cast when they arrive for dress rehearsal.

The society's stage carpenter will take charge of the stage staff unless the resident theatre carpenter is employed for this purpose. The stage carpenter is responsible for setting up and handling the scenery.

It is advisable to use experienced men for the control of staff and lighting. They know how to handle their own men better than an amateur temporarily introduced for this purpose. If the society's carpenter and electrician are experienced technicians, however, they can be used in place of the theatre staff, or arrangements can be made for them to work in co-operation with the resident employees. This is a matter of policy which should be decided upon in the early stages of production.

Thus we have three groups of operatives under the control of (a) the stage carpenter, (b) the electrician, and (c) the property master. These head technicians are responsible to the stage manager for the efficient working of their staff.

THE SCENERY REHEARSAL

The first thing to be tackled on the morning of the dress rehearsal is the setting up of the scenery. This is the stage carpenter's job, and he and his staff will commence work immediately the scenery arrives at the theatre.

In setting up the scenery it is better to work backwards, setting the last scene first, so that Scene 1 can remain set ready for the dress rehearsal.

All items of scenery are as a rule clearly described and numbered on the backs of flats, cloths, borders, etc. They should correspond exactly with the scene plot.

All scenes should be set out in running order in "packs" placed as conveniently near the acting area as possible. That the "packs" are in the right working order is the stage carpenter's responsibility, and this should be done before the rehearsal begins. Clear spaces must be left for dead "packs," i.e. scenery no longer required. Arrangements should also be made to keep forward any pieces or scenes which are repeated.

The centre line of the stage should be established so that borders, backcloths, backings, returns, rostrums, and so on can be accurately set. The line of sight from different parts of the auditorium should be considered, particularly when there is important action at the sides of the stage. Similarly, the height of the borders should be set so that the audience in the gallery and circles have a clear view of the scene. If they are set too low, part of the scene may be obscured from view.

The stage cloth should be set in position first. When all the cloths, flats, rostrums, and other items in the scene have been correctly placed, their positions should be marked on the cloth with chalk or paint. It is necessary to make only small marks at the corners to indicate these positions. A different coloured paint or chalk should be used for each scene.

All borders and cloths should be correctly "deaded," i.e. set level at their correct height. When these positions are fixed, the flymen mark them by tying pieces of string on the lines at a set point where they are secured to the flyrail.

Once the scene is set, the property master and his staff arrange the furniture and other properties relating to the scene. The furniture should be arranged in packs on the same basis as the scenery, so that the pieces are readily available in the proper sequence for the various scenes. When the producer has approved the complete setting, the positions of the furniture and carpets are marked on the stage cloth.

While the scenery is being set the electricians can proceed to deal with any electrical fittings required for the scene, e.g. wall brackets, table lamps, chandeliers, etc.

When the scene has been approved by the producer in every detail, and all positions marked on stage cloth and lines, it can be struck and the setting of the next scene proceeded with in a similar manner.

When the time comes to set the scene again, if the carpenter and property master have done their work properly, all items will be readily accessible and in their correct order. The electrician will see that all fittings are removed or disconnected before the flats to which they are attached are struck.

In supervising the scene changes, the stage manager must arrange the sequence of events so that the different jobs of moving the scenery, furniture, properties, and electrical fittings do not conflict.

THE DRESS REHEARSAL

The dress rehearsal should be allowed to run through, scene by scene, without interruption, apart from the correction of exceptional faults which the producer feels ought to be corrected as they occur. Otherwise there should only be breaks after each scene. The producer and dance producer (or ballet mistress) will have noted the points requiring attention and these should be rehearsed before the scene is changed.

The stage manager will be exercising full control backstage, as he will during the run of the show. He can now time each scene for the last time, allowing for stops, and also the time taken to change the scenes.

The wardrobe department should constantly inspect the costumes from the front during the rehearsal, to assure themselves that all details are correct and that everything fits properly. Similarly, those responsible for hairdressing and make-up should watch the performance to satisfy themselves, and the producer, that their side of the production is up to standard.

If the show has been properly rehearsed, the producer will be able to concentrate on the over-all effect of the show instead of having to struggle with faults and omissions which need not have arisen. The producer who leaves details of this kind to be cleared up at dress rehearsal is asking for trouble, and it will be a tired and disillusioned cast who will make their way home in the early hours of the morning.

The dress rehearsal should not be appreciably below the standard of the opening performance as far as the players are concerned, so that the producer can devote most of his attention to *tempo* and finesse, and to smoothing out the mechanics of the production.

CHAPTER NINETEEN

THE LIGHTING REHEARSAL

THERE is no mystery about stage lighting, nor should it present difficulty, although to the uninitiated lighting equipment does appear complicated. The switchboard, with its conglomeration of controls, the network of wiring and cable, the various circuits, and the groups of spots and floods with their range of colour mediums, present an awe-inspiring array to the producer who is tackling the job for the first time.

The mechanics are not the producer's concern. His job is to use the available equipment to the best effect, and that is a matter of experiment and experience.

THE PURPOSE OF STAGE LIGHTING

Stage lighting is used for several purposes. First, it is used to illuminate the scene so that the audience can see the action. Its second most important function is to give the scene depth and colour by the proper use of the various lighting units—floats, spots, floods, and so on.

Lighting is also used to suggest atmosphere and mood. The grim darkness of a prison cell, the dramatic value of a red sunset, the chill mystery of moonlight and deep shadow, all can be produced and accentuated by clever lighting to give a scene realism. The glow of a forest fire, flashes of lightning, heavy rain, the ripple of water on a lake, and many other mechanically-produced illusions are made possible by means of modern stage-lighting equipment.

A scene does not spring to life until it is adequately lit. The addition of effective lighting is like putting the finishing touches of colour and sunlight to a picture.

To flood a scene with white light is not enough. It is the carefully placed touches of colour, the suggestion of golden sunshine streaming in through a window or lighting up the branches of trees, the crystal clearness of an azure blue sky, the effect of landscape extending into the distant beyond, which, through stage lighting, bring sparkle and interest to the scene.

A musical show is larger than life, and the lighting should conform. With a straight play lighting must be authentic and logical. In a musical play it is permissible to take liberties to produce effects which will enhance the entertainment value of the show at any given point. The use of following spotlights on the principal players, the introduction of coloured lighting effects during a musical number or ensemble, bringing the lights up to full at the end of a number, are typical examples of effects which are fully justified in a musical play.

While the producer should endeavour to get the most artistic results possible with the lighting at his disposal, he should remember that in a musical show a first essential is visibility. Whereas in a straight play it may be effective, in creating a mood through lighting, to play a long scene in semi-darkness, this is rarely advisable in musical entertainment which depends on variety of colour and movement, and swiftly-changing situations. Comedy, for example, should invariably be well lit. The audience will not laugh at something they cannot see clearly, and much may depend upon facial expression and visual humour. Where comedy scenes call for a certain amount of subdued lighting—as in a night scene— this should be designed for visibility as well as effect, and more licence taken than in the case of a straight play.

REHEARSAL PRELIMINARIES

The lighting rehearsal should not be rushed. It is not advisable to hold it during the dress rehearsal when the cast is present, if this can be avoided. If it cannot be arranged before the dress rehearsal it is better to hold it in the afternoon before the opening performance, or in the morning if there is no band call.

The producer should arrange his lighting rehearsal so that he deals with the last scene first, working back to Scene 1, which will remain standing for the opening of the show.

The electrician and lighting staff must be present for the rehearsal in addition to the stage manager. The lighting plot should already be in the hands of the electrician so that he will have had an opportunity of getting the necessary equipment together, and ordering any additional material called for by the plot. Copies of the plot, with the cues, should be supplied to the operator on the switchboard, and to the front-of-the-house spot and lime operators.

The first part of the lighting rehearsal will be concerned with connecting up the various lighting units, and getting them into their positions.

All furniture and other stage properties should be in their positions for each scene.

PROGRESSIVE LIGHTING

Some producers prefer to start with all available lighting on, and then work back from this maximum to the result they require. Others reverse this process, building up intensity and colour methodically from the different mediums in turn. The latter method is, in our opinion, the most satisfactory.

When lighting a musical play it is advisable always to check the final result for each scene from the circle and gallery, where the full effect can be assessed. The stage manager will transmit the producer's instructions to the electrician on the switchboard.

The spot bar is usually set first at the correct height. The various lights—flood and spots—are then focused on the relevant positions on the stage and the required colour mediums inserted. The stage manager can act as a "stand-in" so that the producer may check up on the directional accuracy of the lights. No other lights should be in operation at this juncture, so that the spots and floods on the bar, directed on the scenery or stage to produce touches of colour and sunlight, can be clearly seen and checked before further lighting is brought into play.

Other fixed spots and floods, including acting area floods, should next be brought in and tested.

The backcloth should be dealt with now, and this should be as brilliantly lit as possible. The most satisfactory method is to light it from top and bottom, with supplementary floods at the sides.

If there is a groundrow in the scene the bottom lighting can be obtained by arranging a row of lights behind it. These must not be set too near the backcloth, otherwise much of their lighting value will be lost. The top batten should also be suitably placed to flood the upper portion of the cloth. The side floods should be set sufficiently high on their stands to avoid shadows when the players make their entrances and exits.

When side floods only can be used they must be placed correctly. Nothing spoils a scene more than a badly-lit backcloth. If the floods are placed too near the cloth the light will be concentrated at the sides, leaving the centre in comparative darkness. The oblique beam of light will also show up all the creases in the canvas.

The floods in other entrances and wings should be set next, again taking care to avoid shadows. The positions of all flood stands should be marked when finally placed for the scene.

If there are front-of-the-house spots from the circle these can be dealt with next. The beams from these should be concentrated within the scene clear of the borders and backcloth. If set too high they may produce shadows on the cloth when the players come into the beam.

The floats and battens should now be brought in on the various circuits to the intensity and colour value required. The general effect for the scene can now be adjusted by experiment until the desired result is obtained. Finally the stage spots, pageants, and any other effect lighting should be introduced.

LIGHTING CHANGES

When the basic lighting for the scene is finally set and the positions of all floods duly marked, the rehearsal of the lighting changes can now proceed. When the same scene is used twice, the lighting changes for both occasions can be rehearsed in one session to avoid having to reset the scene.

The electrician will previously have studied the lighting plot, and should have a good idea of the cues and changes involved. Each change should be rehearsed as often as necessary, until the desired result and the mechanics of obtaining it are clearly understood by all concerned. Modifications to the lighting plot may have to be made and these should all be carefully noted. When the rehearsal is over, copies of the final revised plot should be supplied to the electrician and the stage manager.

The lighting plot may include special effects requiring very accurate cueing, and it is worth while spending extra time on these until they are perfect. The operator on the long-distance spots from the projection box can generally be contacted by phone from the stage for instructions. In musical shows it is customary to give a general instruction for following star principals with the spots, and an experienced theatre operator will usually do this with the minimum of detailed information.

The electrician can be of considerable assistance at the lighting rehearsal, provided he has had an opportunity of studying the lighting plot in advance. If he is not given a fair chance, or is dealt with tactlessly, the rehearsal is likely to be both trying and confused, with dire results at the opening performance. The lighting rehearsal should be a tranquil affair of considered experiment, based on a definite plan—the lighting plot. In this atmosphere the producer can successfully complete the pattern of colour, romance, and music he has set out to create.

CHAPTER TWENTY

THE FIRST NIGHT AND AFTER

EVERYTHING should be done to make the front of the house as attractive as possible. This is too often neglected. Photographs of the principals should be displayed in frames outside the house, or in the entrance. The parish hall atmosphere should be eliminated as far as possible. There should also be adequate "billing" on the front of the building which should be properly illuminated. If the show is being presented in a theatre there will be certain facilities for front-of-the-house publicity. If, however, it is being produced in a hall not frequently used for theatrical performances, permission to put up striking posters and special lighting should be arranged if possible. It is surprising what a difference a little showmanship and a suggestion of real theatre atmosphere can make to the success of a show. Some of the dreary approaches to many halls, and their cold uncomfortable auditoriums, are hardly conducive to a gay evening's entertainment.

The box-office should have a courteous and adequate staff to deal with bookings and tickets. Officials of the society detailed for reception duties in front of the house should wear evening dress. The foyer should be bright and inviting. A crowded, brightly-lit foyer is a good advertisement for the show, and, in a busy district, will attract many passers-by.

Arrangements ought to be made to receive, and entertain, the Press and important first-night guests. Inside, ticket collectors and ushers should be available at all entrances in sufficient numbers to show patrons to their seats and sell programmes.

If there is no curtained rail to the orchestra it is worth hiring suitable material to make one. Some expenditure on plants and flowers to brighten up a drab proscenium is also worth while.

The orchestra should be in their places a few minutes before the rise of the curtain. The musical director should be "spotted" when he takes the stand to conduct the overture, the house lights lowered, and the footlights set in accordance with the lighting plot. There is often unavoidable delay on a busy first night in getting the audience into their seats, and a few minutes grace should be allowed before the musical director takes the stand. When he does he should commence the overture (or the National Anthem if this is played before the performance) immediately he gets the cue light from the stage manager. Hold-ups and awkward waits must be avoided and an atmosphere of slickness and efficiency introduced into the proceedings. If the show starts off in this atmosphere it will put the audience in a receptive mood. If the preliminaries are protracted and it looks as if the show will never start, the audience may become bored and restive, to the detriment of the performance.

It is only natural that everyone connected with the production will have first-night nerves. Strangely enough, this can be an advantage provided nothing disastrous is likely to happen through lack of organization. The excitement of a first night keeps the cast up to a high pitch of endeavour, and it is very often the second night which produces the opposite reaction—a tendency to relax which reveals itself in an inferior performance. The producer should seek to forestall this possibility when going over his notes at the end of the show with the cast. This is his last opportunity of suggesting any last minute improvements and of correcting first-night faults. It is unlikely that the cast will be available for a rehearsal call next day, as would be the case with a professional company. The show is now set and there is little he can do to make any drastic changes.

It is surprising how a show suddenly springs to life on a first night in the presence of an audience. The heavy, unresponsive dress-rehearsal feeling disappears as if by magic, and the weeks of hard work at last begin to look as if they have been worth while.

THE VALUE OF CRITICISM

Amateur actors rarely receive reliable criticism. Their public is generally indulgent while the local press, conscious that the company and their friendly patrons are also their readers, are as a rule either over-lavish in praise or cautious and non-committal. This is a pity because it makes it difficult for an amateur company to assess its work accurately. All the more reason why, therefore, if honest criticism is offered it should not be resented but encouraged.

It would be extremely useful for future guidance, for example, if the society could obtain a true consensus of opinion on points such as the following—

Was the show a wise choice?

Was the production up to the expected standard?

Any criticisms of scenery, costumes, furnishings, properties, effects, lighting, make-up, etc.

Observations on the orchestra and musical interpretation.

Comments on *tempo*, groupings, movements, dancing, and chorus work.

Was the show properly cast?

Comments on individual performances.

Did the show build up progressively, or did it have weak patches?

Any special observations on characterization, audibility, and expression.

Did the comedy come over successfully?

Was the production as a whole well balanced?

The resident manager of the local theatre would probably give a constructive criticism of the production if approached in the right way by someone not directly connected with the show, e.g. a vice-president or honorary member.

Whatever the press critic may have written for diplomatic reasons, he may be prepared to unburden his soul and say in confidence what he really thinks, if encouraged by a sensible appeal for constructive criticism off the record.

Above all others, the producer is probably in a better position to offer unabashed criticism if he will only do so. Very often, the question of whether he will be invited to do the society's next production may make him cautious. Again, outspoken criticism might appear to reflect unfavourably on his producing ability. If, however, he has won the complete confidence of the company, and is satisfied that he has done everything humanly possible to get the best work out of them, there is no reason why he should not speak freely. What he has to say will be listened to with respect. After all, if the production and the performances will not stand criticism, they must have been bad indeed. In presenting a sincere and unbiased assessment of the show from the producer's viewpoint he will be doing the society a real service.

The amateur operatic movement has long ceased to be a mere social pastime. To-day its standards are high, its contribution to national music and drama considerable. A number of entirely new works have been performed for the first time by amateur societies. Still more could be done in this direction. British authors and composers, long neglected, might find new hope and encouragement through the enterprise of the amateur movement. There is a great opportunity here for adventure and experiment which should not pass unheeded.

LIST OF LIGHT OPERAS AND MUSICAL PLAYS SUITABLE FOR AMATEUR PRODUCTION

(BEFORE deciding on any musical show, societies should contact the copyright owners in order to ascertain whether the amateur performing rights will be available at the time of production.)

COPYRIGHT OWNERS (KEY TO ABBREVIATIONS)

ASCHERBERG . . Ascherberg, Hopwood & Crew, Ltd., 16 Mortimer Street, London, W.1.

BOOSEY . . . Boosey & Hawkes, Ltd., 295 Regent Street, London, W.1.

CARTE . . . D'Oyly Carte Opera Co., 1 Savoy Hill, London, W.C.2.

CHAPPELL . . Chappell & Co., Ltd., 50 New Bond Street, London, W.1.

CRAMER . . J. B. Cramer & Co., Ltd., 139 New Bond Street, London, W.1.

CURWEN . . J. Curwen & Sons, Ltd., 24 Berners Street, London, W.1.

DANCE . . . George Dance Musical Plays, 63/65 Piccadilly, London, W.1.

ELKIN . . . Elkin and Co., Ltd., 20 Kingly Street, London, W.1.

FRENCH . . Samuel French, Ltd., 26 Southampton Street, London, W.C.2.

G. & T. . . Goodwin & Tabb, Ltd., 36/38 Dean Street, London, W.1.

HAYS . . . Alfred Hays, Ltd., 74 Cornhill, London, E.C.3.

KEITH PROWSE . Keith Prowse & Co., Ltd., 42 Poland Street, London, W.1.

LITTLER . . Emile Littler Musical Play Dept., Palace Theatre, Shaftesbury Avenue, London, W.1.

M. & Y. . . Macdonald & Young, Emanwye House, Bernard Street, London, W.C.1.

N.O.D.A., LTD. . N.O.D.A., Ltd., 8 Bernard Street, London, W.C.1.

PLADIO . . . Pladio Ltd., Abbotts' Chambers, 202 Bishopsgate, London, E.C.2.

S. & B. . . . Stainer & Bell, Ltd., 58 Berners Street, London, W.1.

WILLIAMS . . Joseph Williams, Ltd., 29 Enford Street, London, W.1.

TITLE	COMPOSER	COPYRIGHT OWNERS (OR CONTROLLERS OF PERFORMING RIGHTS)
Ali Baba	West	Curwen
Aladdin and Out	Hewitt	Curwen
Aladdin in the Underworld	Rowley	Boosey
Amasis	Faraday	Cramer
And So To Bed	Ellis	French
Annie Get Your Gun	Berlin	Littler
Anything Goes	Cole Porter	French
Arcadians, The	Monckton and Talbot	French
Arlette	Jane Vieu	N.O.D.A., Ltd.
At the Silver Swan	Samuels and Mackay	French
Balalaika	Posford	French
Balkan Princess, The	Rubens	Dance
Barbara	Clutsam	Chappell
Beauty Prize, The	Kern	Littler
Beauty Stone, The	Sullivan	Carte
Beggar's Opera, The	Austin	Boosey
Belinda Fair	Strachey	French
Belle of Brittany, The	Talbot	French
Belle of New York, The	Kerker	French
Beloved Vagabond, The	Glass	Ascherberg
Betty	Rubens	Littler
Betty in Mayfair	Fraser Simson	French
Bitter Sweet	Coward	French
Bless the Bride	Ellis	French
Blossom Time	Schubert–Clutsam	French
Blue Eyes	Kern	French
Blue Kitten, The	Friml	M. & Y.
Boy, The	Monckton and Talbot	Littler
Brigands, The	Offenbach	Boosey
Cabaret Girl, The	Kern	Littler
Careless Rapture	Novello	French
Carissima	May	French
Castles in Spain	Brae	French
Castles in the Air	Wenrich	M. & Y.
Catherine	Tchaikovski	Littler
Chieftain, The	Sullivan	Carte
Chinese Honeymoon, A	Talbot	Dance
Chu Chin Chow	Norton	French
Cigale, La	Audran	Ascherberg
Cigarette	Parry	Cramer
Cingalee, The	Monckton	Dance
Cloches de Corneville, Les	Planquette	Williams
Count of Luxembourg, The	Lehar	Littler
Country Girl, A	Monckton	Dance
Cox and Box	Sullivan	Carte
Cupid and the Ogre	Hector	Curwen
Dancing Mistress, The	Monckton	Littler

Title	Composer	Copyright Owners (or Controllers of Performing Rights)
Daughter of the Gods	Talbot	N.O.D.A., Ltd.
Dear Love	Haydn Wood, Tunbridge and Waller	M. & Y.
Dear Miss Phoebe	Parr-Davies	Littler
Derby Day	Reynolds	Elkin
Desert Song, The	Romberg	French
Desert Wings	Hill	N.O.D.A., Ltd.
Devil Take Her	Benjamin	Boosey
Dogs of Devon	Bullock	Curwen
Doris	Cellier	Chappell
Dorothy	Cellier	Chappell
Duchess of Dantzig, The	Caryll	Dance
Earl and the Girl, The	Caryll	French
Emerald Isle, The	Sullivan and German	Chappell
Eunice	Veitch	N.O.D.A., Ltd.
Falka	Chassaigne	Hays
Fallen Fairies	German	Chappell
Fille de Madame Argot, La	Lecocq	Boosey (No performing fees)
Fille du Tambour Major	Offenbach	Cramer
Five O'Clock Girl, The	Ruby	M. & Y.
Fledermaus, Die	Johann Strauss	N.O.D.A., Ltd.
Florodora	Stuart	N.O.D.A., Ltd.
Frederica	Lehar	N.O.D.A., Ltd.
Funny Face	Gershwin	M. & Y.
Gaiety Girl, A	Caryll	N.O.D.A., Ltd.
Gay Parisienne, The	Caryll	Dance
Gay Romance	Palmer	G. & T.
Geisha, The	Jones	Littler
Gipsy Baron, The	Johann Strauss	N.O.D.A., Ltd.
Gipsy Love	Lehar	Littler
Gipsy Princess, The	Kalman	N.O.D.A., Ltd.
Girl Friend, The	Rodgers	M. &. Y.
Girl from Kays, The	Caryll	Dance
Girl from Utah	Jones and Rubens	Littler
Girls of Gottenburg, The	Caryll and Monckton	Littler
Glamorous Night	Novello	French
Golden Moth, The	Novello	Littler
Gondoliers, The	Sullivan	Carte
Good-night Vienna	Posford	French
Grand Duchess, The	Offenbach	N.O.D.A., Ltd.
Grand Duke, The	Sullivan	Carte
Greek Slave, The	Jones	Littler
Gretchen	Silver	Curwen
H.M.S. Pinafore	Sullivan	Carte
Haddon Hall	Sullivan	Carte

Title	Composer	Copyright Owners (or Controllers of Performing Rights)
Happy Day, The	Rubens and Jones	Littler
Harmony Hill	Glass	N.O.D.A., Ltd.
Havana	Stuart	Littler
Her Ladyship	Talbot	Chappell
Here Comes the Bride	Schwartz	M. & Y.
Highwayman Love	Bullock	Curwen
Hit the Deck	Youmans	M. & Y.
Hold Everything	De Sylva, Brown and Henderson	M. & Y.
Hong Kong	Jessop	Chappell
Hugh the Drover	Vaughan Williams	Curwen
Immortal Hour, The	Rutland Boughton	S. & B.
Iolanthe	Sullivan	Carte
Irene	Tierney	M. & Y.
Island King, The	Garstin	Littler
Ivanhoe	Sullivan	Chappell
Jack O'Diamonds	Gay	M. & Y.
Jill Darling	Ellis	French
Jolly Roger	Leigh	Boosey
Kamaldar	Hector	Curwen
Katinka	Friml	M. & Y.
King of Cadonia, The	Jones	Dance
King of Sherwood	Hewitt	Curwen
King's Minstrel, The	Coope	N.O.D.A., Ltd.
Kitty Grey	Barratt and Talbot	Dance
Lady Be Good	Gershwin	M. & Y.
Lady Madcap	Rubens	Dance
Lady of the Rose, The	Gilbert	Littler
Lady Slavery, The	Crook and Others	Dance
Land of Smiles, The	Lehar	N.O.D.A., Ltd.
Last Waltz, The	Oscar Straus	Littler
Let's Make An Opera	Britten	Boosey
Lilac Domino, The	Cuvillier	M. & Y.
Lilac Time	Schubert-Clutsam	Chappell
Lisbon Story, The	Parr-Davies	Chappell
Little Dutch Girl	Kalman	Chappell
Little Michus, The	Messager	Dance
Love at the Inn	Quilter	Ascherberg
Madame Favart	Offenbach	Ascherberg
Madame Pompadour	Fall	Littler
Magyar Melody	Posford and Grun	French
Maid of the Mountains, The	Fraser Simson	Littler
Maritza	Kalman	French
Marriage Market, The	Jacobi	Littler
Masquerade	Posford	French

Title	Composer	Copyright Owners (or Controllers of Performing Rights)
Me and My Girl	Gay	French
Mercenary Mary	Friedlander and Conrad	M. & Y.
Merchant Prince, The	Sterling Hill	N.O.D.A., Ltd.
Merrie England	German	Chappell
Messenger Boy, The	Caryll and Monckton	Littler
Mikado, The	Sullivan	Carte
Mirette	Messager	Chappell
Miss Hook of Holland	Rubens	Dance
Missing Heir, The	Forbes Milne	Curwen
Mr. Cinders	Ellis and Myers	M. & Y.
Mr. Pepys	Bax	Cramer
Monsieur Beaucaire	Messager	Ascherberg
Mountaineers, The	Somerville	Ascherberg
Mountebanks, The	Cellier	Carte
Mousmé, The	Monckton and Talbot	M. & Y.
Music in The Air	Kern	Chappell
My Lady Jennifer	Partridge	Curwen
My Lady Molly	Jones	N.O.D.A., Ltd.
Nadgy	Chassaigne	Hays
Nautch Girl, The	Solomon	Dance
Nell Gwynne	Planquette	Cramer
New Moon, The	Romberg	Chappell
Night in Venice, A	Johann Strauss	N.O.D.A., Ltd.
Nina Rosa	Romberg	French
Nippy	Mayerl	M. & Y.
No, No, Nanette	Youmans	French
Oh! Letty	Sharon	M. & Y.
Old Chelsea	Tauber	French
Olivette	Audran	Chappell
Once Aboard the Lugger	Rowley	Boosey
Our Miss Gibbs	Caryll and Monckton	Littler
Our Peg	Fraser Simson	French
Over She Goes	Mayerl	N.O.D.A., Ltd.
Paganini	Lehar	N.O.D.A., Ltd.
Paris in Spring	Lee	Curwen
Patience	Sullivan	Carte
Paul Jones	Planquette	Ascherberg
Pearl the Fishermaiden	Ward	Curwen
Peggy	Stuart	Littler
Pepita	Lecocq	Chappell
Pepys, Mr.	Shaw	French
Perichole, La	Offenbach	Boosey
Phillida	Hector	Curwen
Pink Champagne	Strauss–Grun	French
Pirates of Penzance	Sullivan	Carte
Please Teacher	Waller and Tunbridge	M. & Y.
Polly	Austin	Boosey

Title	Composer	Copyright Owners (or Controllers of Performing Rights)
Poupée, La	Audran	French
Pride of the Regiment, The	Leigh	Boosey
Prima Donna	Benjamin	Boosey
Primrose	Gershwin	Littler
Princess Charming	Szirmai and Bennett	M. & Y.
Princess Ida	Sullivan	Carte
Princess of Kensington, A	German	Chappell
Quaker Girl, The	Monckton	Littler
Rainbow Inn	Strong	French
Rebel Maid, The	Phillips	Chappell
Rio Rita	Tierney	French
Rip Van Winkle	Planquette	Chappell
Rose Marie	Friml	French
Rose of Araby, The	Morgan	French
Rose of Persia, The	Sullivan	Carte and M. & Y.
Rose of the Border	Elliott Smith	Ascherberg
Royal Exchange	Horan	French
Ruddigore	Sullivan	Carte
Runaway Girl, A	Caryll and Monckton	Littler
San Marino	Silver	Curwen
San Toy	Jones	Littler
Shop Girl, The	Caryll	Littler
Show Boat	Kern	Chappell
Silver Patrol	Thayer	French
Silver Wings	Waller and Tunbridge	M. & Y.
Song of Norway	Grieg	Chappell
Song of the Sea	Kunneke	French
Song of the South	Ross	N.O.D.A., Ltd.
Sorcerer, The	Sullivan	Carte
Southern Maid, A	Fraser Simson	Littler
Sporting Love	Mayerl	N.O.D.A., Ltd.
Springtime	Hillier	N.O.D.A., Ltd.
Stand Up and Sing	Charig and Ellis	French
Street Singer, The	Fraser Simson	French
Student Love	Brahms–Spurgin	French
Student Prince, The	Romberg	Pladio
Sunny	Kern	Chappell
Sunshine Girl, The	Rubens	Littler
Sunshine of the World	Cuvillier	M. & Y.
Sweet Yesterday	Leslie-Smith	French
Sybil	Jacobi	Littler
Sylvia's Lovers	Rolt	Chappell
Tantivy Towers	Dunhill	Cramer
Tell Me More	Gershwin	Littler
1066 and All That	Reynolds	French

Title	Composer	Copyright Owners (or Controllers of Performing Rights)
That's a Good Girl	Charig and Mayerl	French
Three Graces, The	Lehar	Dance
Three Little Maids	Rubens	Dance
Three Musketeers, The	Friml	Chappell
Tina	Rubens	Littler
Tom Jones	German	Chappell
To-night's the Night	Rubens	Littler
Toreador, The	Caryll and Monckton	Littler
Trial by Jury	Sullivan	Carte
Tulip Time	Wark	French
Two Bouquets, The	Irving	French
Utopia Ltd.	Sullivan	Carte
Vagabond King, The	Friml	French
Véronique	Messager	Dance
Vie Parisienne, La	Offenbach	Boosey
Viktoria and Her Hussar	Abraham	French
Virginia	Waller and Tunbridge	M. & Y.
Waltz Dream, A	Oscar Straus	Dance
Waltz Time	May	Keith Prowse
Waltz Without End	Chopin–Grun	French
Waltzes from Vienna	Johann Strauss	Chappell
Whirled into Happiness	Stolz	Littler
Who's Hooper?	Talbot and Novello	Littler
Wildflower	Youmans and Stothart	Pladio
Wild Violets	Stolz	Chappell
Yeomen of the Guard, The	Sullivan	Carte
Yes, Madam	Waller and Tunbridge	M. & Y.
Young England	Clutsam and Bath	Ascherberg

THEATRICAL SUPPLIERS

COSTUMES, WIGS, AND MAKE-UP

Morris Angel and Son, Ltd.,
117–119 Shaftesbury Avenue, London, W.C.2.
Uniforms. Modern and period dress for men. Period costumes for
ladies.

R. Sheldon Bamber, Ltd.,
12–13 Charing Cross Mansions, Glasgow, C.3.
Costumes and wigs.

"Bert,"
46 Portnall Road, London, W.9.
Make-up artist and wigmaker. Wigs available for hire.

B. and H. Drury, Ltd.,
23 New Road, Brighton.

Fashion Hire, Ltd.,
7 Short's Gardens, London, W.C.2.
Ladies' modern costumes.

Chas. H. Fox, Ltd.,
184 High Holborn, London, W.C.1.
Costumiers and wigmakers.

W. A. Homburg, Ltd.,
31 Call Lane, Leeds, 1.
Costumiers and wigmakers.

Leichner (London), Ltd.,
32 Acre Lane, Brixton, London, S.W.2.
Make-up Studios, 11 Great Newport Street, London, W.C.2.
Manufacturers of make-up and cosmetics.

William Mutrie and Son, Ltd.,
Proscenium House, Bell's Brae, Dean Bridge, Edinburgh, 4.
Costumes and wigs.

L. and H. Nathan, Ltd.,
12 Panton Street, London, S.W.1.
Costumiers and wigmakers.

B. J. Simmons and Co. (1941), Ltd.,
7 King Street, Covent Gardens, London, W.C 2.
Theatrical costumiers.

F. A. Smith, Ltd.,
All Saints, Manchester, 1.
Costumiers and wigmakers.

Stage Furnishings, Ltd.,
426 and 450 Sauchiehall Street, Glasgow.
Costumes, wigs, and cosmetics.

Theatrical Suppliers,
268 Rockingham Street, Sheffield, 1.

Alfred Turner Stage Shoes, Ltd.,
76 Stretford Road, Manchester, 15.
Ballet, tap, and chorus shoes.

S. B. Watts and Co.,
18–20 New Brown Street, Manchester, 4.
Theatrical costumiers.

RECORDED SOUND EFFECTS

Bishop Sound and Electrical Co., Ltd.,
48 Monmouth Street, London, W.C.2.

The Strand Electric and Engineering Co., Ltd.,
29 King Street, Covent Garden, London, W.C.2.

SCENERY

R. Sheldon Bamber, Ltd.,
12–13 Charing Cross Mansions, Glasgow, C.3.

Cape,
Sutton Lane, Chiswick, London, W.4.
Portwood Works, Corporation Street, Stockport, Cheshire.

Dodsworth and Spencer,
Wellington Road Studios, Undercliffe, Bradford.

B. and H. Drury, Ltd.,
23 New Road, Brighton.

James Fredricks Scenic Studios,
8 Elmhyrst Road, Weston-super-Mare.

Bert Loman Studios, Ltd.,
Bloomsbury Hall, Rusholme Road, All Saints, Manchester.

William Mutrie and Son, Ltd.,
Proscenium House, Bell's Brae, Dean Bridge, Edinburgh, 4.

Northern Contractors, Ltd.
147–9 Northumberland Street, Newcastle-upon-Tyne, 1.

Scenic Display Services, Ltd.,
Norcroft Studios, Listerhills Road, Bradford.

Stage Furnishings, Ltd.,
426 and 450 Sauchiehall Street, Glasgow.

Stage Scenery, Ltd.,
13 Short's Gardens, Monmouth Street, London, W.C.2.

A. Whyatt and Son,
Grand Theatre, Wolverhampton.

STAGE EQUIPMENT AND FURNITURE

Hall Manufacturing and Supply Co., Ltd.,
Wynne Road, London, S.W.9.
All kinds of stage equipment. Parts and material for scenery
construction.

Old Times Furnishing Co.,
125A, Victoria Street, London, S.W.1.
Furniture, carpets, curtains, stage draperies and properties.

PROPERTIES

Robinson Bros. (Jewellers), Ltd.,
 6 Hampstead Road, London, N.W.1.
 Properties and effects machinery.
Stage Properties,
 33 Great Windmill Street, London, W.1.
Robert White and Sons,
 57–59 Neal Street, Shaftesbury Avenue, London, W.C.2.
 Jewellers, armourers, and swordmakers.

STAGE-LIGHTING EQUIPMENT

W. J. Furse and Co., Ltd.,
 82 Traffic Street, Nottingham, and at London, Manchester and
 Bristol.
 All types of lighting equipment for sale and hire.
The Strand Electric and Engineering Co., Ltd.,
 29 King Street, Covent Garden, London, W.C.2., and at 399 Oldham
 Road, Manchester; 62 Dawson Street, Dublin.
 All types of lighting equipment for sale and hire.

PUBLICITY MATERIAL

Potten, Baber and Murray, Ltd.,
 75–78 Milk Street, Bristol, 2.
  Colour designs for programmes, window cards, folders, car screen
  bills, postcards, throwaways, etc.
Ridge Studios,
 50 Crouch Hall Road, Crouch End, London, N.8.
  Programme covers, cover blocks, etc.
Stafford and Co., Ltd.,
 Netherfield, Nottingham, and 55 Berners Street, London, W.1.
  Posters, window pictorials, programmes, postcards, folders, day-
  bills, etc.

INDEX